Laughing for a Living

for a

By

Sue Merrell

Cover photo by Kym Reinstadler. Publicity photos supplied for "Some Like It Hot," "Damn Yankees," "Nunsense," Mickey Rooney, James Earl Jones and Cary Grant. Julie Newmar photo by permission of The Post and Courier, Charleston South Carolina.

ISBN 978-0-557-72893-0

Laughing for a Living

Most Thursday or Friday nights for the past decade, I could be found hard at work—laughing in an aisle seat.

As a theater reviewer for The Grand Rapids Press in Michigan, I have spent much of my professional life laughing and watching other people laugh. We all dream of doing work we love. Other professions may provide a greater sense of accomplishment, more financial reward, and higher acclaim. But I can think of no other field—save that of a wine taster, perhaps—in which enjoyment is the object of the job, the measure of success.

When it comes to laughing, I'm a pro. At least people tell me I have a distinctive laugh—not the cackle of the Wicked Witch, exactly, but the kind of robust laugh that's contagious, the kind of laughter comedians like to hear. In Charles Dickens' time, they paid people to wail at funerals. I probably could make a profession out of filling the audience with contagious laughter, if I wasn't already getting paid to be objective and critique the shows. And there's the rub. Critics have a reputation of being sourpusses who never like anything, probably because cutting barbs are much more fun to read than syrupy praise. But I love theater, from the weird, indie pieces that barely make sense to the Broadway standards I've seen too many times to count.

Of course, there are a few pesky details, such as researching the facts and meeting deadlines, which seldom inspire a smile or a snicker. Nevertheless, a good chunk of my workday—actually "work evening," since most performances are at night—was spent having a good time and making notes in the dark theater to record the causes of my joy.

The notes themselves were pretty funny and almost always unreadable. Theaters are dark. I would scrawl a word or two on the page, unable to see the lines. When I wanted to make another comment, I'd have to guess where the last comment ended. Most of the time I guessed wrong and wrote on top of the previous scrawl. But it usually didn't matter. The very attempt to put down my thoughts seemed to impress the moments on my memory. It's like all those notes I took in college but never studied after class that somehow echoed in my mind on test day.

"You get paid to do this?" people often asked incredulously.

I have to admit it was pretty amazing to earn a living doing something I would gladly do for free. Live theater has been my favorite entertainment since I was a little girl growing up near St. Louis, Missouri. And even though I saw more than 50 plays a year on the job, I spent my vacations going to Broadway or the Stratford Festival in Ontario, Canada, to get another fix of my favorite drug. I can understand why my predecessor, David Nicolette, reviewed Grand Rapids theater for 40 years, up until a few months before his death at age 80.

When I wasn't sitting in the best seats in the house at the opening of a hot new play or concert, I was interviewing the stars before they got to town or "studying," ie poring over every little detail of the stars' lives, like a teenage groupie.

"How does somebody get a job like that?" was another frequent question. Well, I came up through the reporter ranks, taking birth announcements and then wedding announcements, before moving on to the weekend cops beat, then covering school boards, park boards, planning commissions and city councils. But I stumbled into interviewing stars 36 years ago, and it eventually mushroomed into my specialty.

I came to Grand Rapids in 1990, after eight years as assistant city editor at a much smaller newspaper in Joliet, Illinois. I was hired as assistant features editor, supervising day-to-day operations for features and entertainment. I functioned as unofficial entertainment editor until our rock music reviewer, John Gonzalez, took over those reins five or six years later. I tired of my job in the late 1990s and interviewed for jobs in Florida as sort of a preretirement move. About that time, we were trying to find a theater reviewer to replace Dave, but none of the people we interviewed seemed right to me. Then it suddenly hit me: I should take that job and let them hire someone to replace me as assistant features editor.

It turned out to be the best decision of my life.

"I know I have the best job in the building," I told Press editor Mike Lloyd when I decided to retire early in 2009. Although I'm being weaned gradually while continuing to write about theater on a freelance basis, I know my life of laughter has been too perfect to let it fade away without sharing a few behind-the-scenes stories. Such as meeting master comedian Jerry Lewis and seeing his rude and angry side. Or finding out that quintessential charmer Cary Grant was a little paranoid. Imagine having to put up with Tony Curtis rubbing your leg or Bette Midler calling you at home. And you'll never believe the shape secret of Julie Newmar that I kept under wraps for 36 years!

Laughing for a living has been fun and frightening, at times. Sad and silly. Inspiring and irritating. But dull? Never.

Tony Curtis in a scene from the stage musical "Some Like it Hot"

"I haven't had plastic surgery. Just retin-A and the saliva of beautiful girls."

Some Like It Hot

I realized I was officially an old-timer when Grand Rapids Press Entertainment Editor John Gonzalez e-mailed me the morning after actor Tony Curtis died in September 2010.

"Got a second?" the e-mail began, as if that's all it would take for me to turn on my memory and spew out a story about the time Curtis visited Grand Rapids. John wanted to get a story online as soon as possible to catch the spike in Google hits. It would be repeated in the next day's paper.

I wasn't exactly on the clock anymore. I had been retired more than a year. But I couldn't blame John. Many times, when I was in his position, I went to the previous theater critic, David Nicolette, and asked him to "localize" a wire story about the death of someone famous. It was a little jarring, however, to know I had become the go-to person for movie-star obits.

Tony Curtis was the sex symbol of my youth, back when all I knew of sex was symbols. He was sooooo cute. He invented the pretty boy pout long before Elvis, who supposedly stole the idea for his sculpted hairstyle from Curtis.

I could give you a list of his movies, but he appeared in 137 from 1949 to 2000. Suffice it to say, he was in so many movies in the late '50s and early '60s that I thought his name was a permanent part of the movie marquee. I jumped at the chance to interview him when he came to Grand Rapids in 2003 with a stage version of his 1959 movie, "Some Like It Hot."

Broadway tours often include a ringer, someone with name recognition who may end up with a fairly small part but gets star billing nevertheless. Like Jerry Lewis in "Damn Yankees" or Eartha Kitt in "Cinderella," Curtis was the name that was selling "Some Like It Hot."

In the movie, Curtis and Jack Lemmon played young musicians who witness the St. Valentine's Day Massacre and have to escape Chicago. They dress up like women and join a female band headed for Florida. In the musical, Curtis played the much smaller role of Osgood Fielding Jr., a wealthy man who falls for one of the musicians masquerading as a woman.

"I get to sing and dance and chase women—my life's work," Curtis told me in a phone interview before the show arrived in town. "I've got a feeling that's why they got me to do this role. Typecasting."

Although Curtis had been married five times and his current wife was 45 years younger, I didn't realize what a flirt he was until I met him. Media from the Grand Rapids television stations and the Chicago Tribune had gathered in a suite at the Amway Grand Plaza in downtown Grand Rapids for 15-minute slots with the star. Like many of the celebrities I've met, the 77-year-old Curtis showed up dressed for photos of the top half only. From the waist up he was a polished professional with a nice black shirt and lush, curly white hair (which I soon figured out was a wig). On the bottom half he wore loose-fitting, wrinkled white shorts and sandals, even though it was January and below freezing outside. This split-personality dressing is pretty common at press conferences. It's as if stars are purposely rebelling against the image they are expected to project. They want the media to see the "real" person, but they don't want the rest of the world to know. Or maybe being half comfortable and half business is its own statement.

A makeup person followed Curtis around, keeping his hair and face perfect for every camera, while the star took charge of the room. He greeted everyone—cameramen, lighting techs, interviewers. He asked every name, shook every hand. He kissed women's hands or gave them a peck on the cheek. He wasn't shy about telling photographers how to place lights to avoid casting shadows on his face, and he would loudly announce "Quiet on the set!" when a television interview was about to begin.

Like a gracious host, he made the rounds between interviews, chatting and smiling. He really seemed to enjoy the buzz of people swarming all over the suite. But he simply couldn't keep his hands to himself.

Our interview took place at one end of the living room area with him sitting in a chair and me seated at right angles to him on the sofa. I was wearing black crepe slacks and a white sweater with a white fur collar. There was snow on the ground, so under my slacks I wore knee-high, black stretch-vinyl boots, which peeked out when I crossed my legs.

In the middle of my interview, Curtis reached out and touched one of my boots, as if he wanted to see if it were leather. I was shocked. I stopped whatever question I was asking. Curtis was obsessed with my boots, rubbing my calf and pushing back my slacks to examine the boots more closely.

Soon I dropped my planned questions in favor of comparing my winter footwear to his shorts and sandals. He said he liked to show off his legs, which were as smooth and shapely as a woman's. He said a woman once stopped him in Las Vegas where he lived and said, "I'd recognize those legs anywhere. It's Tony of the movies."

Curtis kept rubbing my leg and saying how much he liked my boots. Now, you have to understand, this man was only a year younger than my father, and although his gorgeous hairstyle made him seem much younger, there was a soft transparency to his skin that reminded me of my Dad, whose health was failing at the time. I felt a sort of respectful patience with the actor's forward behavior, a willingness to overlook his harmless, if inappropriate actions.

I didn't consider it sexual harassment. I wasn't really offended by his interest in my boots. I didn't feel threatened in any way, because the room was buzzing with lots of people. If anything, I guess I felt embarrassed. It was an odd and unexpected experience.

I remained in the suite after my interview was over. I listened as Curtis did his television interviews, making notes of off-hand comments and noticing his interaction with others. Between interviews, Curtis came over to where I was standing near the doorway. He rubbed his fingers over my fur collar.

"You feel just like a little bunny rabbit. I could take you home with me."

Okay, so that's pretty overt flirting, but I didn't take him seriously. He seemed to have similar conversations with other women in the room. I couldn't overhear exactly what he was saying to the other women, because he would move in close, keeping the interchanges small and intimate, personal comments meant only for the woman to hear. Flirting, for him, seemed almost compulsive.

"I haven't had plastic surgery," he said when complimented on his fairly unwrinkled skin. "Just retin-A and the saliva of beautiful girls."

When I finally decided to leave, I stopped by to thank the female publicist who had arranged the interview opportunity. Curtis came up and draped an arm around each of us, saying how much he was enjoying visiting with everyone. Then just as I was leaving, he brushed a hand across my cheek.

"You have such beautiful skin," he said.

Well, I'm not exactly Miss America, and I know it. But to have Tony Curtis tell you that your skin is beautiful—even if you're certain he must have said that to at least a dozen women in the past hour—goes to your head in a wonderful way. I walked back to the office crunching snow under my boots, but I was blushing like springtime.

A Little Thief

When I was a toddler, an adult asked me if I could stand on my hands.

"I think I can," I replied with a child's optimism.

I bent over, lifted the toes of my shoes just enough to put my fingers underneath and "stood" on my hands.

My family repeats that story often. It's one of the many stories we tell on each other and laugh. I grew up in one of the happy families that Leo Tolstoy said are all the same and therefore not worth writing about. But to be honest, I think my charmed career as an entertainment journalist began in that boring, happy home where parents and grandparents doted on my every word and action

I'm the oldest of four children, but my father was an only child, so I was the first grandchild in the Merrell family. The day before I was born in St. Louis, my parents moved into the upstairs half of a two-family flat owned by my grandparents, who lived downstairs. Thus, my reign began.

My grandmother gave me my first role in a

church Christmas production when I was 3 years old. She taught me a little poem:

"What can I give Him, poor as I am?

"If I were a shepherd, I'd give a lamb,

"If I were a wise man, I'd do my part,

"But such as I have, I give my heart."

I recited the words with the emphasis Grandma had taught me, and everyone said I stole the show. When I heard that, I cried.

"But Grandma, I didn't steal anything."

I was bitten, however, by the acting bug. We moved to a St. Louis suburb in Illinois, and I was always writing and directing little plays for my brothers and friends to perform in the living room. We had a big picture window with drapes, so I would set up a few lawn chairs on the porch where our parents could sit. One of us would open the curtains, another would drop the needle on the little record player, and we'd all sing or dance or just act silly for the applauding audience looking in through the window.

Leading my brothers and neighbors in a parade performance

I do remember, however, a particularly nasty bout of stage fright when I was in first grade. I was in some sort of all-school program in the high school gymnasium, which seemed enormous to a 6-year-old. The first-graders gathered in the locker room under the bleachers and my parents were in the audience above. I'm not sure if I started crying or turned pale or what exactly happened. I only know my classmates headed on stage without me. When I didn't come out, my mother came looking for me. She found me in the locker room with one of the teachers. A motherly hand to the forehead gave the quick diagnosis of fever and by the time I got home I had sprouted the telltale spots of measles.

I ran a high fever that night—104 degrees, I think—and had horrible hallucinations of the angry crowd coming after me because I failed to participate in my class performance. I was better in a day or two but had to remain at home for a week. In those days, children with measles were advised not to watch television because it was believed to damage the weakened eyes. My mother sat me in one of her high-back chairs, turned away from our little black-and-white television, so I could hear, but not see, "The Howdy Dowdy Show."

Through the years, those chairs were passed on to me. Nicely reupholstered, they sit next to my flat screen TV as a constant reminder of my stage fright initiation.

The highlights of my childhood were summer trips to the Muny Opera in St. Louis, where I saw my first live musicals, such as "Pajama Game," "Auntie Mame" and "Seven Brides for Seven Brothers."

During high school, I was in every play, either onstage or backstage. In "The Adventures of Tom Sawyer," I played Aunt Polly, walking on stage as the curtain opened and yelling "Yooo, Tom" loud enough to win the state hog-calling contest. My brother, whose name happened to be Tom, crawled under his seat.

I sang "We Love You Conrad" in "Bye Bye, Birdie," modeled an atrocious gown as Myrtle Mae in "Harvey" and went to the state drama contest with my scene from "Arsenic and Old Lace."

I continued to act during the first two years of college—as Toinette in "The Imaginary Invalid" and Cary in "Barefoot in the

Park"—and took all the theater classes I could find. But when I entered journalism school at the University of Missouri in my junior year, I put away childish things like acting in plays. It was time to get serious about a field of study that might actually lead to a job. I liked writing, and Mark Twain said the best way to learn to write was to work for a newspaper. So, I got a degree in journalism, never dreaming I someday would be able to write about my first love—theater.

Although I continued to watch live theater as often as I could, it would be 25 years before I returned to the stage—after divorcing my husband of 12 years, raising a son on my own, working at four newspapers and living in seven states.

My church in Kentwood, Michigan, announced a production of "Cheaper By the Dozen," and I had to audition. One of the authors, Frank Gilbreth, had been the business manager at one of the papers where I worked, the News & Courier in Charleston, South Carolina. His daughter, Betsy Moye, had been my editor. I was cast as the strict teacher, Miss Brill. Returning to the camaraderie on the other side of the curtain reminded me that performers don't steal shows; the show steals the performers.

Theater will always have a corner of my heart.

BAND-AID® Test

What do you wear to interview a movie star? Even the most confident person probably would give the matter some thought. But if you didn't know you would be interviewing a star, you might have shown up as I did that April morning 36 years ago, dressed for casual Friday long before it was in vogue. I was wearing a navy blue polyester pantsuit with high-water pants. I can't explain why I would wear pants that were too short, especially since I had made the outfit and should have been able to adjust the length. Nevertheless, those should-have-been-longer pants were my first thought when my editor, Betsy Moye, told me I would be interviewing Julie Newmar.

Actually, "interview" wasn't exactly my assignment.

In 1974, the News & Courier and Evening Post were separate papers operating out of the same building in downtown Charleston, South Carolina. I worked for the women's department that served both publications. Newmar, who was Catwoman on the "Batman" television series and Stupefyin' Jones in the "Li'l Abner" movie, was a friend of our publisher, Peter Manigault, and was in town for a visit.

A popular columnist for the morning paper had been assigned to interview Newmar and write the main story for the next day's paper. As the newbie in the women's department, I was to write a "second-day" story—not as big, but offering some information about the visit—for readers of the afternoon paper. The whole event was arranged at Middleton Place Gardens, where our photographer could get some good pictures and the columnist could record Newman's reaction to the beautiful Southern landscaping. My instructions were to write a story based on what I could observe and overhear from the columnist's interview. Basically, I was supposed to stay out of the way.

I tried to fade into the background in my ill-fitting pantsuit. My plan worked well for a while. Newmar and the columnist sat down for an interview while the photographer and I wandered around. I tried to overhear what I could from their conversation without interrupting, but it wasn't much.

Then it was photo time, and we returned to the van to pick up a change of clothes for Newmar—a beautiful floral chiffon dress in turquoise and lavender with a huge turquoise hat and silk shoes to match. She was going to change in the restroom, and since I was the only other female in the party, I was recruited to help carry the dress and accessories.

The ladies room was in a small building at the edge of the gardens with only a stall or two. Performers usually are not modest types, since they often change costumes hurriedly in the wings, so I wasn't surprised that Newmar planned to change in the restroom's common area rather than one of the cramped stalls. We stationed the photographer outside to guard the door.

I didn't have a spare hand for pen and pad, but holding the hanger with the long dress over my head, I chatted casually with the star, who eagerly described her "Charleston Dress." Making and designing her own clothes had become a necessity for the 6-foot-2 statuesque beauty.

"I have to be unique. I don't want to look like anyone else," she told me.

Her grandmother had taught her to sew, and she made her own clothes for a few years, but once she became a star, she employed two seamstresses to turn her ideas into reality. She already had worn the Charleston dress to the premiere of the film "The Great Gatsby." I didn't mention that I also made my own clothes, as I tugged at my slacks, trying to cover my ankles.

"A graceful woman is a Southern woman; a feminine woman is a Southern woman. Why shouldn't I be a Southern woman?"

The chiffon dress was a wrap with a plunging neckline, but Newmar didn't have to worry about her bra showing because she wasn't wearing one. When she disrobed, I found myself eyeball-to-nipple with the naked chest of Stupefyin Jones. I couldn't help but notice her matching set of racing stripes—3-inch transparent adhesive bandage strips placed vertically about 1 inch above the nipple of each breast.

"What happened?" I blurted before my natural editor could kick in. I thought perhaps the lithe 40-year-old actress had breast implants or had undergone some other surgery, such as for breast cancer.

With a laugh, Newmar explained she was wearing the bandages instead of a bra, and she patiently showed me how the adhesive strips had been applied strategically to pull the skin taut over each breast. It was rather like tightening the straps on an invisible bra. They provided a little lift, restoring the perkiness of a 25-year-old without disguising the natural, sexy shape of her breast.

Well, there's nothing like sharing an underwear secret to break the ice. For the rest of the afternoon, Newmar treated me like an old friend as she posed for pictures on the beautiful terraced lawn and prowled the garden paths. She posed amid the greenery and flowers, trying to evoke the image of a Southern woman, even though she was born in California, lived in New York and spoke with British enunciation.

"A graceful woman is a Southern woman; a feminine woman is a Southern woman," she said. "It has nothing to do with where you were born. Why shouldn't I be a Southern woman?"

She joked around and tried to get me to pose for pictures with her, but I declined. We giggled over jokes I don't recall. When people recognized her and wanted autographs, I shared my pen.

But when the visit ended, I feared I still didn't have enough usable comments to do my story, so I asked her if I could have just five more minutes. We stepped inside a darkened barn, and I asked her how she felt about her sex-symbol image. It was a time of women's liberation and the Equal Rights Amendment. Did she regret that she was often cast for her body instead of her talent?

"I'm delighted to be thought of as a sex symbol," she said. "I will be even more delighted to be considered a sex symbol when I'm 70. I like to be thought of as a vital, lively person. Sexuality is energy; that's all it is."

At this writing, Newmar is 77 and still being invited to strut her stuff at comic book conventions. In addition to acting in numerous movies and television shows, she made money investing in real estate and has been working on writing books. She even holds three U.S. patents for her body-shaping creations. (Can you patent a new use for adhesive strips?)

Newmar's name has become so synonymous with being a sex symbol that it was featured in the title of a 1995 drag-queen movie, "To Woo Fong, Thanks for Everything, Julie Newmar" That title always makes me laugh, because about a week after my piece ran, Newmar called me at the Post-Courier office and thanked me for the story. If she'd sent an autographed photo, the inscription probably would have sounded a lot like the movie title. But I was tickled with the phone call. She confided that she liked my story better than the bigger one written by the much more experienced columnist. I knew she'd probably told him she liked his story the best, but I basked in her praise anyway.

My first interview with a movie star was a success.

Lady Elvis

I was surprised the first time I saw Tanya Tucker in 1974. I had read about the 15-year-old country music phenomenon in Newsweek magazine. She had her first country hit record, "Delta Dawn," at age 13 and already had won Top New Female Vocalist at the Academy of Country Music Awards. When I saw that she was the opening act for Ray Price at Charleston's Municipal Auditorium, I arranged to interview her backstage after the matinee and before the evening performance.

Arrangements were made by calling her father, Beau Tucker. I talked to him on the phone one evening from my kitchen. I imagined him sitting in a farmhouse kitchen somewhere in the Tennessee area code I'd been given. Later I realized he probably was calling me back from a dressing room at another show or some motel on the road. Beau was Tanya's road manager, and her brother was driving the bus and managing the lights. I imagined families in the three-bedroom ranch of my life, not the bus-and-bar world Tanya knew.

So, I was surprised to see this 15-year-old appear on stage in a skin-tight gold lame costume that was every bit as sexy and sultry as her deep voice and provocative moves. After her act, I headed backstage, found Beau and was directed up a narrow stair to a small dressing room high above the wings.

Tanya had changed into a T-shirt and jeans and was removing makeup at a little dressing table in the corner. I was struck by how she went about her business without a mother or assistant. Not even her dad was standing by to monitor the interview. Tanya was in charge.

Looking and acting beyond her years was part of the appeal.

"Many of my songs speak of things people think a young girl shouldn't know about," Tanya said with a big smile. One of her recent hits, "Would You Lay with Me in a Field of Stone," was considered a "dirty song" by some people, she said.

"But it actually expresses wedding vows and you'd have to love a person quite a lot to do what that song asks. Maybe someday I'll use it in my wedding."

As she answered my questions, Tanya brushed out her shoulder-length blond hair, divided it with a casual part down the center of her head and caught a handful of hair in a rubber-band pigtail behind each ear. Now she looked 15.

Her music idols were Merle Haggard and Elvis Presley, she said. None of the female singers were idols, she said, because she considered herself on the same level with female singing stars.

"But there isn't any woman who is popular the way Elvis is. That's what I want to be."

Elvis died just a few years later, overweight and on drugs. Tanya went through her own hard times with drugs and alcohol. But she kept on singing, kept on recording, kept on performing. She may never have reached a status anywhere near the King of Rock 'n' Roll, but in 2002, Country Music Television named her one of the 40 greatest women of country music, and in 2009 she still was recording albums. My favorite song has always been "Two Sparrows in a Hurricane" because it reminds me of that 15-year-old girl who had a dream.

"She's 15 and he's barely driving a car," it begins.

"Like two sparrows in a hurricane
"Trying to find their way
"With a head full of dreams
"And faith that can move anything,
"They've heard it's all uphill,
"But all they know is how they feel.
"The world says they'll never make it,

"Love says they will,"

"The girl in the box office turns you in, and before you know it, everyone is watching you instead of the movie."

Blowing in My Ear

Cary Grant hung up on me.

I know it's not a very gentlemanly thing to do and Cary Grant is the consummate gentleman. That's why I couldn't believe it.

Now, it pains me to imagine that someone reading this may not know who Cary Grant is, but since he released his last movie, "Walk, Don't Run," more than 40 years ago, I have to admit it's possible that generations will never know the most handsome and debonair actor who ever lived. Born in England as Archibald Leach, he started out as an acrobat and mime. Fluid grace and physical expression crowned every role he played.

I've probably seen at least half of the 72 movies he made. My favorite was "An Affair to Remember," a heartbreaking love story with Deborah Kerr. Remember the sentimental movie Meg Ryan was watching in "Sleepless in Seattle?" That was "An Affair to Remember."

In September 1986, Grant was touring theaters with a one-night show called Conversations with Cary Grant. He'd play some movie clips, tell a few stories and answer questions from the audience.

Naturally, I was excited when I heard he'd be coming to the Rialto Square Theatre in Joliet, where I was assistant city editor at The Herald-News. One of my responsibilities was the Sunday Entertainment section, which I figured gave me dibs on the one interview being offered to the press. But Grant was such a cultural icon that the Herald-News' columnist, John Whiteside, thought he should do the story. I seldom needed to compete for an assignment, but I wasn't going to let this one slip through my fingers. It was a once-in-a-lifetime chance to speak to Cary Grant, for Pete's sake! I was relieved when the city editor said the assignment was mine.

Interviewing a celebrity requires a great deal of preparation. I read three books about Grant from the public library and watched every video I could find. The interview was scheduled for 10 a.m. California time—noon in my office in Illinois. When I called the number I had been given, a woman answered, but soon he came to the phone. In the casual prequestion banter, he asked me about the pronunciation of Joliet (Not Jolly-et) and recalled he had visited the beautiful old Rialto Theatre in the early part of his career, when he was doing pantomime.

Being the suspicious journalist I am, I worried a little that the person on the other end of the phone line could have been anyone, an assistant perhaps. An impersonator. But there was just something about his voice, the way he pronounced the "i" in "idea" and "might." It was really him!

Then all of a sudden he said, "What's that? Are you blowing in my ear?"

Before I could clarify what he had heard, he hung up. I panicked. I certainly didn't have enough for my story. So, I dialed the number again and prayed he would answer. He did.

"Someone picked up the phone and was listening in," he said. "Someone in your office knows about the interview."

I had a hard time convincing him that the office was almost empty for the lunch hour, and the few people still at their desks had no idea what I was doing. Besides, our lines in the office were separate. No one could listen in, except possibly at his house. And so what if somebody DID hear what he said? It was going to be published anyway.

The interview was fine from there on, but I was sorry to have my image of this perfect man marred by that moment of petty paranoia. He was 82 at the time. I worried that his paranoia might be an indication of Alzheimer's or some other serious condition.

As he answered my questions and told his stories, I could see some basis for his fear. He could never go shopping or go to a movie theater, he said, because he was too recognizable.

"The girl in the box office turns you in, and before you know it, everyone is watching you instead of the movie," he said.

I was really impressed that in the 35-minute phone conversation, he never spoke ill of anyone. He never criticized an inept director or snooty leading lady. He spoke of his four ex-wives —Virginia Cherill, Barbara Hutton, Betty Drake and Dyan Cannon —with respect and said all his marriages were happy at the time. His current wife, Barbara, was mentioned with almost reverence.

"A man rushes about trying to prove himself," he said. "A woman just has more wisdom."

Nothing's sexier than a man who loves his wife.

Grant said his only regret was his impatience with autograph hounds and pushy fans. "I regret not being gracious," he said.

I know, I know. He was giving me Miss America answers calculated to paint a picture of a personality as flawless as his face. And I gobbled it up.

A few months later, I was working the copy desk one Saturday night when a news bulletin moved on the wire. Cary Grant had been taken to a hospital in Davenport, Iowa. He had collapsed onstage while preparing one of his Conversations with Cary Grant.

For the next couple of hours, I watched as the story developed. Midnight: A bulletin moved that a cardiologist had been called; 1 a.m: An unconfirmed report of his death.

It wasn't one of the evenings when my job inspired laughter. That night, as the slotman or chief of the copy desk, it was my job to clear out a space in the newspaper for the story, which didn't get confirmed until a few minutes after our 1:30 a.m. deadline. But I made the necessary changes and got the story and the photo on Page 1 for the Sunday morning paper.

And all the time while I was working, I kept hearing his melodious voice echoing in my memory. On Monday, a reporter from People magazine called to ask me about my interview with Cary Grant, one of the last before his death. I didn't tell her about him hanging up on me and his paranoia that someone might listen to our conversation.

It didn't seem gracious.

Gone with the Wind

Like the night Cary Grant died, much of my work has been anything but funny. My first real story was covering a tornado that hit Eagle Pass, Texas, in 1972. I was living in Del Rio, where my husband was in pilot training for the U.S. Air Force. I did a little writing for the Del Rio News Herald, mostly routine clerical stuff such as birth announcements. One morning when I came in, the editor said a tornado had hit Eagle Pass, about 60 miles southeast of Del Rio, the previous evening. He told me to ride down with the photographer and write the story.

The photographer was a thin, white-haired woman who was about as prickly as a cactus and just as tough. I remember she had huevos rancheros—spicy scrambled eggs wrapped in a tortilla—in one hand, an equally hot cup of coffee in the other and a big camera bag over her shoulder. I don't know how she managed to drive her pickup truck and continue eating her two-fisted breakfast, but she did, probably because staying on the road is optional in Texas since the ground is as hard as the pavement.

There wasn't much to see between Del Rio and Eagle Pass, but as we got closer to the town, we began to see strips of corrugated aluminum twisted like giant curled ribbons littering the road and the surrounding landscape. Telephone poles were sheared in half and more aluminum ribbons dangled from the wires that remained.

Then we saw a trailer park with all the trailers flattened. As the photographer took pictures, I wandered around. It was an odd mixture of order and chaos. The walls were missing from one kitchen, but an open package of pork chops lay on the kitchen counter as if the storm had interrupted dinner preparations.

I could hear a cat mewing somewhere beneath the rubble. The photographer and I searched but never found the frightened pet.

More than a decade later, I was running the copy desk one Friday evening at the Joliet Herald-News when a tornado struck the town. Sirens were blaring and phones were ringing.

"If you look out the window right now, you can see it," a caller told me.

I turned, and there on the horizon, moving across the dark storm clouds, was a jagged white line. It was thin and slanted to the ground. It almost looked like a lightning bolt frozen on the clouds. I stood open-mouthed at the windows, watching as the 60-degree line wiped across the horizon.

"Shouldn't we be getting under desks or something?" one of the sportswriters asked.

But the white tornado wasn't heading toward us, and it soon disappeared. I radioed the photographer, John Patsch, and sent him to the site of an overturned trailer I had heard about on the police scanner. I called him back a minute later and asked him to detour into a neighborhood where a caller said his garage had been carried away.

John, a large man of few words, radioed back about five minutes later.

"They're gone," he said.

"Who's gone?" I asked.

"The houses. They're gone."

The tornado ripped up any previous plans we had for the next morning's paper. John returned with award-winning pictures of people emerging from basements to find their entire neighborhood gone. Six injuries had been reported but no one was killed.

A caller who had snapped a picture of the storm cloud brought in his film and it ended up front and center in our photo display.

Reporters who had gone home for the day reported back to work to help write the stories.

No one was laughing that night, but there's an adrenaline high in horror and tragedy that's strangely exhilarating. It gave us the energy to work and when the work was done, I was exhausted.

I was a single mother then and thankful that my son was out of town, safe at his grandmother's. I went home to bed in the wee hours of the morning, pleased that the paper had done justice to a difficult story. The next morning, neighbors told me they had watched as the tornado passed through open fields about a block from my house.

Covering theater doesn't usually lead to life-and-death disasters, but once in Grand Rapids I was pulled in to do a story on an explosion because the survivor was one of the actors I had covered many times. One of the advantages of beat reporting is that you develop trust among the sources you cover on a regular basis. The survivor declined to speak to our police reporter but agreed to speak to me.

"You can drop a house on me like I'm the Wicked Witch of the West, and I crawl out from under it," Neil Trevisan joked the next morning from his home on Grand Rapids' northwest side. Trevisan had played such roles as Captain Hook in "Peter Pan" and Dr. Frank-N-Furter in the "Rocky Horror Show."

Trevisan had called the gas company to report the smell of gas at his hair studio, which was one of the tenants in a large building in a neighborhood just east of downtown. When the gas company representative arrived, Trevisan volunteered to go back into the building and show him the door to the basement.

"He had a meter in his hand," Trevisan told me, "and said something like, 'Getting a reading here.' Just as he said it, boom! I mean, like, movie-special-effects boom. It was so instantaneous, so catastrophic. It took us a minute to catch up to what had happened."

Although the explosion destroyed the building, Trevisan and the other people still inside escaped with minor injuries.

"It's a miracle I didn't have any appointments at that time," he said. "I'm just glad that I had that little break. If I had an appointment, I would have been up there doing someone's hair and I would be dead. And she would be dead, too."

Open Sez Me

My job has taken me into worlds most people never see. I've been in a nuclear power plant, a monastery and a crumbling Southern plantation that survived Sherman's march. One of the most memorable places I visited was a fantastical factory full of candy-making machines covered in a cloud of white fairy dust— with a 6-foot mountain of bubble gum in the corner. I know it sounds like something out of that 1971 movie, "Willy Wonka and the Chocolate Factory," but in real life that's exactly what I found when I toured Amurol Products in Naperville, Illinois, a few years after that movie came out.

"The air smells sweet, a bit like grapes," I reported in the Aurora Beacon-News.

"Past glistening machines churning out a parade of brightly colored packages, past a pyramid of rainbow-hued candies, past a pantry of serrated sheets of confections, there is a mountain of bubble gum. It is a pink, jagged mountain sprinkled with a white powder something like fairy dust.

"Huge jaws stir the gooey gum as white-coated men make additions from a palette of colors and flavors. The fairy dust snow-drifts on some of the machines as they whir, smoothing and shaping the gum into sticks and logs. Footprints of fairy dust follow you everywhere."

Actually the fairy dust was a starch, which kept the sticky product from literally gumming up the works. Amurol was started in the mid-1940s by a group of dentists to make tooth powder, but in the 1950s they started offering sugarless gum. Since the goal was to prevent cavities, they wanted something that appealed to kids and created the first sugarless bubble gum, Blammo! When I did my tour in the late 1970s, my guide predicted sales would burst the billion-dollar bubble by 1980.

But the funniest part of the whole tour was meeting the panel of chemists—we're talking multiple degrees on the wall—who sit around blowing big pink bubbles to "test" the product's "film strength." I kid you not. And you thought I had a cushy job.

On the opposite end of the fantasy spectrum, I also toured Stateville Correctional Center, the maximum security prison most people think of when they hear the name "Joliet."

About a dozen reporters and editors from The Herald-News took a tour of the facility, which houses about 3,000 major criminals. I couldn't help but be impressed by the buildings – the towering cellblocks, gymnasium, painting class, even a theater group. We were touring an empty cafeteria, listening to our guide point out the security posts for armed guards high above the room, when I noticed one of the reporters looking out the back door of the cafeteria into the hall. He waved over a co-worker, and pretty soon our guide was talking to himself. Our reporter had spotted Richard Speck in the hall, painting the wall.

Speck, you may recall, was a famous mass murderer who killed eight student nurses in a Chicago flat in 1966. (He died of a heart attack in 1991 about two years after our tour.)

Without questioning what had attracted our interest in the hall, the guide proceeded with his tour and soon led us out into the hall where Speck was on painting detail. We fell into single file as we walked past the scaffolding. Just as we passed, Speck reached for a roller on the end of a long broom handle, and as he swung it around, every woman in our group ducked.

And the reporter who had recognized him in the first place? He dawdled behind the group and handed Speck his card—in case he ever felt like talking to the press.

Hard at Work

Perhaps the most outrageous thing I've done in the guise of work is driving drunk. And to make it even crazier, I drove drunk with an Illinois State Highway Patrolman in the passenger seat.

The patrolman, who handled publicity for the area State Highway Patrol post, had stopped by the Herald-News office to drop off a news release and we got to talking.

"Do you drink?" he asked.

Talk about a loaded question. What do you say when a patrolman with one of those big Smokey Bear hats asks a question like that?

Driving drunk with Smokey.

"A little," I hedged.

He invited me to participate in a demonstration set up at an area hospital to show nurses, insurance agents and members of the media what it feels like to drive drunk. There were eight or 10 of us, and it started off at about 9 a.m., very businesslike. They let each of us pick our poison—I ordered rum and coke—and they served me a double.

As we sipped our drinks, they showed us charts about the effects of alcohol on our bodies and the number of drunken driving accidents. After 20 minutes, each of us blew into the Breathalyzer. I was already .04, about twice as drunk as the other participants and a little less than halfway to being legally drunk in Illinois. Then we drove a course that had been set up in the parking lot with bright orange pylons. It was a snap. This drinking and driving is easy. But two drivers hit pylons along the course.

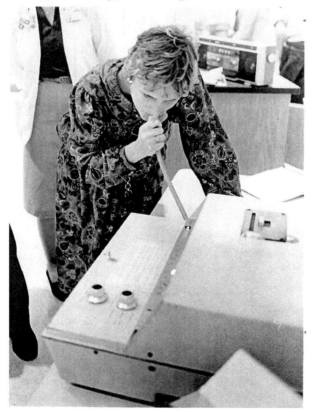

Then we repeated another round of doubles. Nobody was pointing out numbers on charts any more. We were just laughing. Everything was so funny. The next time we visited the Breathalyzer, I was .08, legally drunk in some states and very near the Illinois limit. I was double most of the other participants, probably because I was the shortest member of the group and had skipped breakfast.

"Isn't your liver working?" the trooper asked.

I definitely was impaired at this point, and I hit one of the pylons when driving the course. But you know, I didn't care. I thought it was funny. I suppose if I'd been driving on the road instead of a parking-lot course, that pylon could have been a mailbox or a dog or even a child.

After the next round, my liver finally kicked in and I blew .09, still shy of the legal limit in Illinois, but the other participants had caught up to me by now. This time I lost points for driving too slow. Too slow? I could barely walk or hold up my head. I just wanted to lie down. I remember laying my head and upper body across the Formica table. The trooper told me I could quit because I was clearly uncomfortable, but you can't expect a person who is .09 to be wise enough to know when it's time to quit.

"No," I insisted without raising my head from the table. "I have to hit 1.0" Judging by how much the troopers laughed, I must have slurred my words a bit.

After the fourth double, I had hit the magic legal limit. But by then it was raining and the driving exercise was canceled. The photographer took me home. It was barely noon and I was passing-out drunk. When my son arrived home from school, he found me asleep on the sofa, but I had already arranged for a neighbor to watch him until I sobered up.

The next day I wrote a story about the experience.

"At first I was disappointed in the test. I had expected some graphic demonstration of the drunk driver, pylons flying everywhere. But it didn't happen. Drunk driving, I found, is much more subtle. A drinking driver continues to drive fairly well; not as well as a sober driver, of course, but the failings are not blatant enough to convince the driver not to drive. Instead, the ability to continue to function gives the drinking driver false confidence. So what if you hit a pylon, now and then? Or a mailbox? Or a dog? Or a child?"

This general store in Horton Bay is one of Michigan's northern sites that Ernest Hemingway mentioned in his stories.

It seemed almost like spying to find notches measuring the heights of the Hemingway children etched into a doorframe.

Up North

One of the best ideas I ever had was an Up North travel column. When I moved to Grand Rapids, I noticed how people kept talking about going "Up north." I soon figured out that about 150 miles north of Grand Rapids was the weekend getaway of choice. Towns like Traverse City, Petoskey and Charlevoix have been summer attractions for more than a century. Chicagoans, such as Ernest Hemingway's family, traveled by ship and train to get to these magical, woodsy towns dotted with pristine lakes.

I started dating a guy who was a charter-fishing captain in one of the most picturesque little towns—Leland. I would go up to see him on weekends, and while he was working a charter, I had plenty of time to explore the attractions. I was assistant features editor at the time, and the travel section was in my department, so I launched a biweekly column about the places so many people from Grand Rapids visited, from Legs Inn restaurant in Cross Village to Gwen Frostic's print shop in Benzonia.

Oh, what I went through for that column! One weekend I tested not one but two relaxing spa treatments. I received a hot stone massage at Bay Harbor and a cherry honey glow treatment at Grand Traverse Resort. I was so relaxed when I returned to work on Monday morning, I was still floating in a dream state.

Grand Traverse Resort has a 100,000 square-foot spa complex with two indoor pools, five indoor tennis courts and 11 multipurpose treatment rooms.

"I thought I had stepped into the holodeck on the Starship Enterprise!" I wrote in my column. The cherry honey glow treatment is a sort of salt scrub followed by a Vichy shower.

"Now if you've never heard of a Vichy shower, the sight of six shiny shower heads hanging over your massage table can look a bit sterile and frightening. But just think how good that morning shower feels on your back, then multiply that pleasure by six and you get the idea."

The hot stone massage was even more relaxing. I had to sit in the lobby for 20 minutes after my treatment to be sure I wouldn't fall asleep at the wheel.

Another weekend I squeezed in two sailing adventures on Grand Traverse Bay, comparing West Bay's beloved tall ship, The Malabar, with a racy little catamaran, Nauti-cat, on East Bay. More than a decade later, I can remember the ecstasy of the sun and the wind on those delightful afternoons. All I had to do to pay my passage was to come up with the words to describe it

"There's plenty of room for passengers to mingle, stretch out in the sun or just enjoy the melody of the flags flapping in the breeze," I wrote about the Malabar. *"Every 20 minutes or so, at the captain's command, the mates rustle about adjusting the sails to tack for the return trip."*

The Malabar was shipshape, but the Nauti-Cat was the naughtiest ship on the Great Lakes, the captain boasted, as he and his first mate lobbed biodegradable water balloons across the path of jet skiers who were violating the rules of right-of-way.

For three years I spent every other weekend in the summer finding new ways to have fun, from the Buckley Old Engine show to afternoon tea at Busha's Brae, an herb garden. I wrote about the elusive Petoskey stone, fossilized coral that is found on northern beaches. I sought tips for finding the even more elusive morel mushroom. A month before the annual Mesick Mushroom Festival, I stopped into a bar in the small northern town and asked the bartender if he could direct me to the best mushroom hunter around.

"That'd be me," he said, puffing his chest out with pride.

I read Hemingway's "Torrents of Spring," his toss-off novel that was set in Petoskey, and visited the sites mentioned in the book. The rooming house where he lived a few months bears an emblem as a National Historic Site. The cottage on Walloon Lake, where the Hemingway family spent many summers when the author was a boy, is hidden from the public except on rare tours. Hemingway's nephew, Ernest Hemingway Mainland, welcomed me into the cottage, which still has many of the furnishings of the early twentieth century. It seemed almost like spying to find notches measuring the heights of the Hemingway children etched into a doorframe.

Perhaps my most extravagant Up North adventure was dining at the gourmet restaurant Tapawingo—on The Press' tab.

This is fine dining in a quiet atmosphere of simplicity, with the emphasis on excellent food and service. The wait staff was there instantly with an hors d'ouevre and reset the table for each course with exactly the implements needed. Our first courses were fantastic, as we had been lead to expect. My main course, a filet of beef with potato and corn ragout, was decorated with an orange flower, an edible nasturtium.

And then the perfect meal suddenly went awry.

An ant crawled out of the tropical-looking flower and ran across my plate. I was simply horrified. Of course, it wasn't the first time in my life I've had an ant on my plate, but the other times were on camping trips or at picnics—not in fancy restaurants with fancy price tags. And I wasn't responsible for writing about it.

My friend, Steve, noticed my horror as the pesky ant made his way off my plate and across the tablecloth.

"What ant?" Steve said crushing the invader with his thumb. "I don't see an ant."

He thought I could just go on as though it never had happened, but I couldn't. I knew I would have to address the topic in my story and I didn't know where to begin. I choose not to mention it to the staff. I didn't want someone bringing another plate of food. But my appetite was ruined.

Later, I called the owner, chef Pete Peterson, who explained an occasional ant is the price of using fresh flowers. I handled it just that way. A simple explanation from the chef. But whenever someone mentions edible flowers, I know the ants have first dibs.

Unintended Consequences

Sometimes I stumbled into a story when I wasn't expecting to find one, and sometimes the impact of a story was hard to predict.

Early in my career I noticed a classified ad in the News & Courier for a belly dancing class that sounded intriguing. I signed up. The class turned out to be in a ranch style house in a typical family neighborhood with all these ordinary housewives lined up in the garage, jingling from the bells on their belts and the tiny cymbals on their fingers. It was too good a story to pass up.

Students in the class ranged from teenagers to grandmothers. A secretary, a computer programmer, housewives and a beautician all signed up for a fun type of exercise. One "domestic engineer" who hadn't seen her Navy husband for six months, had lost 60 pounds since starting the class and learned some sexy moves.

"If that doesn't shock him, nothing will," she told me.

The teacher was tickled with the free publicity my story provided, and her garage soon was jingling several hours a day, six days a week. But the city's zoning officer read the paper, too. The teacher received a notice that her class was in violation of the zoning rules, so she had to rent a studio in a more appropriate commercial district to continue offering classes. Renting a studio was a big step for her; it wasn't just her silly garage project anymore. But she rented a studio, put up a sign and took out a bigger ad.

When the cowboy band Riders In the Sky was performing at Van Singel Fine Arts Center in Byron Center in 2003, I decided I wanted to interview Grand Rapids native Fred LaBour, who was the bass player for the group. I have to confess I really wasn't familiar with the group or their style of music. Reporters can't be experts on everything, but we are experts at finding out about everything. While researching LaBour on the Internet, I came across a Fred LaBour about the same age who played a significant role in creating the Paul-is-dead rumor that surrounded the Beatles in 1969.

Now I was interested! The Beatles did my kind of music, and I was very familiar with the death rumors. Remember how there were supposed to be "signs" in their album "Abbey Road?" The cover supposedly represented a funeral march, and remember that line in "The Glass Onion" that said, "the walrus is Paul?" That was another sign, the rumors said, because walrus is Greek for corpse or something like that. Yes, I knew all the signs, but I didn't know they first appeared in The Michigan Daily, a student newspaper at the University of Michigan. The student who wrote that article was the same Fred LaBour who is now a comic cowboy.

"I just made it up," LaBour told me in a phone interview. "I wrote a satirical album review. I concocted this whole scenario. I claimed to have inside information about Paul's death and made up all these clues that were in the album."

LaBour said he was surprised when his story was picked up by papers in Detroit and Chicago and then on both coasts.

"You'd think they could have sent me a fruit basket or something for all the records I sold," LaBour quipped. "I put 'Abbey Road' over the top."

My interview grew into two stories: the advance for Riders in the Sky and a revival of a very famous—but false—rumor.

Another story that grew way out of proportion was the death of a circus horse named Velasquez. I'm not usually on the veterinarian beat, but when a glorious 14-year-old palomino dropped dead at the Ringling Brother's Circus in 2004, it caused such a fuss you would have thought he was Paul McCartney.

Circus employees were unloading the train the day it arrived in Grand Rapids. One of the horses charged another, and the one that was charged dropped dead. The circus provided a basic release of those facts, which I rewrote for the paper. That seemed like enough for me.

But, representatives of People for the Ethical Treatment of Animals claimed that the horse's death was an indication of abuse or mismanagement of animals on the tour. There had been other accidents, other animals had died, which probably isn't too amazing considering how many animals were on the tour.

The palomino's remains were taken to Michigan State University where veterinarians performed an autopsy and discovered the horse had died of a ruptured artery from the heart, which must have happened when Velasquez was charged by the other stallion.

For the next several days, my editor had me calling veterinarians and the health department, even though there was little to report. You know, inquiring minds and all that.

After the third story rehashing the issues, one of the editors left a little plastic horse on my desk and a certificate for the "Beating a Dead Horse" award.

Coffee Break

Perhaps this is a good time to let you in on a little secret—I hate coffee. I detest the smell of it, and if I were nibbling a box of chocolates and bit into a mocha crème by mistake, it would be enough coffee taste to trigger my gag reflex.

I tell you this so you will understand. Sometimes I had to drink coffee in the line of duty, a necessary evil to keep the conversation rolling.

The first time caught me unawares. Charleston Air Force Base had a new commander, and my editor in the women's department at the News & Courier wanted an interview with the general's wife. My editor thought I was perfect for the assignment since my husband was in the Air Force. I was familiar with the base and base housing where the general lived. And I had the necessary sticker on my car to gain easy access to the base. But there's a huge chasm between a lieutenant's wife and a general's wife. Fraternizing with the wife of such a superior officer was probably against military regulations, so, I never mentioned my military connection when I set up the interview.

When I arrived, I was amazed at how much the quarters resembled other base housing, although they were a little larger. A maid or housekeeper showed me into a little breakfast room off the kitchen. The general's wife welcomed me at a little table set with delicate china and a plate of perfectly iced petit fours.

After a few words of greeting, the general's wife poured two cups of coffee from a little china coffee pot. She didn't ask if I wanted coffee, she only asked if I wanted sugar and cream.

"Yes, lots," I thought.

I dawdled over doctoring my drink, and tried to keep the questions coming and my pen writing so it wouldn't seem too strange that I hadn't taken a sip. But when she became concerned that my coffee was getting cold, I had to take a sip and assure her it was just fine. I continued taking occasional sips just to keep the conversation comfortable. I could only hope I wasn't turning as green as I felt.

Several years later, when I was covering general assignment in Geneva, Illinois, I again found myself cornered into drinking coffee. It was my job to stop by the fire station every morning to see if there had been any fires or ambulance calls, but the guys were pretty close-mouthed. This was the mid-1970s and firefighting was still a man's game. A female reporter was about as welcome in the firehouse as a girl would have been in their boyhood treehouse.

One morning, when I stopped by to check the fire log, the chief spotted me from the nearby kitchen and invited me to join him for a cup of coffee. It was an opportunity to break the ice and I had to take it. The kitchen was an industrial, no-frills operation, with a big stove and refrigerator, a sink and a long counter along one wall containing a huge coffee pot and rows of white ceramic mugs. In the center of the room was a 15-foot table covered with red-checked oilcloth. The police department was right next to the firehouse, so men from both departments were gathered around the table laughing and talking almost any time of the day.

For the next two years, when I stopped by the station, I went to the kitchen and poured myself half a cup of coffee. Then I wrapped my hands around the big white mug so I wouldn't be tempted to pull out my notebook, which tended to throw a kink in conversation. I just listened.

I got a lot of good tips around that table—and managed to get by with taking very few actual sips of that smelly black goo everyone else seems to enjoy so much. As the years have passed and I have become more confident—some would say obstinate—I've been able to decline offers of coffee and never felt pushed into drinking it again.

But when I think back to the firehouse kitchen, I have to admit it was worth it. The fire chief became comfortable enough with me that he invited me into fire scenes. I remember an apartment fire at which he welcomed me into the blackened, acrid-smelling ruins and showed me where the fire had started, in a waste can, and the intensely charred area that led him to believe an accelerant had been used.

One morning in the kitchen, I overheard the men discussing a radio-dispatched Santa. Turned out the fire chief had dressed up in a Santa suit to visit the families of his firemen. He was dispatched to various homes via the handheld radio the men used.

I knew I had stumbled into a nice holiday story. The only problem was I needed a photo. I did what a reporter should never do—I staged a photo opportunity. The fire chief was willing to put the Santa suit on again, but I needed children in the picture. I called a neighborhood daycare center and asked if it would be okay if I stopped by with Santa and a photographer. Of course, they were delighted.

The kids were only excited for a few minutes, however.

"What did you bring me?" they started asking.

"Don't you have candy canes or something?" the daycare leader asked. "Santa always brings something."

Silly me. I thought Santa was enough of a treat.

It was horrible. We managed a photo or two, but some of the kids were crying. We figured we'd better cut our losses and get out of there. As soon as we got back into the car, the fire chief asked if he might stop by a nearby nursing home and visit his aunt, who had never seen him in Santa suit.

Although the chief insisted later that it had been a spur-of-the-moment idea, I've always suspected he knew the effect Santa would have at the nursing home. The minute he stepped through the door, eyes that had been clouded over for years lit up.

"Oh, Santa, it's been so long since you came to see me," one shriveled old lady in a wheelchair said.

We ended up going room to room, taking pictures and spreading cheer. Everyone was delighted to see Santa, and no one asked, "What did you bring?" The good stories are always the ones you don't plan.

What's in a Name?

Most of my career, I wrote under my married name, Sue Wallace.

I recall the first time I ever used the name when I ordered a pizza on my honeymoon. The guy on the other end of the phone line asked for a name to put on the order and out of habit I said "Merrell" but quickly corrected myself.

Sue Wallace wrote a consumer column, Buy the Way, for the News & Courier. Soon after our son was born, Sue Wallace became the food editor at the Aurora Beacon-News creating a whole new section of columns such as Dollar Signs, which featured recipes pegged to that week's grocery specials, and Check Out Line, with a team of readers testing various products.

Even after I divorced, I kept my married name because I was raising a son with that last name and it just seemed easier. So, Sue Wallace wrote a singles column for the Herald-News for eight years. You'd be surprised how many single people are out there, almost half of all adults. And when I was writing that column, I met them everywhere. When I picked up my suit at the dry cleaners, the clerk would start telling me about her dating problems as soon as I gave my name. When I used my charge card at J.C. Penney's, I heard about the saleswoman's child custody battles. Even a firefighter who came to my door collecting for charity, launched into a tirade about divorce laws as soon as I signed my name on his clipboard and he recognized me as "the gal who writes that column in the paper."

As an assistant editor for The Grand Rapids Press, my name was kept pretty much out of the public eye, until one day the owner

of a local art gallery became upset with me. He wanted to pick which art reviewer would write about the art in his gallery. I insisted that decision was mine. So, he painted a sign across the windows of his gallery, "Sue Wallace, Grand Rapids Press, You Still Don't Get It." And suddenly people were asking for the story behind the sign, even when I was just cashing a check in the grocery store. Some people pay attention to names.

As I approached 50, I decided to change back to my maiden name. My son was 21. We no longer needed to share the same last name.

My brothers were shocked that I wanted to make a change 16 years after my divorce. "Your life is almost over," one brother said.

I called the circuit clerk's office to see what I needed to do to legally change my name and discovered that my birth name is always legal. I used a birth certificate to change my driver's license and everything else was willing to go with what was on my driver's license.

I changed my byline on the Up North column in increments, going from Sue Wallace to Sue Merrell Wallace and eventually dropping the Wallace. The internal phone log at The Press listed me as "The Editor Formerly Known as Wallace," a play on "The Artist Formerly Known as Prince."

For my 50th birthday, my parents and I visited The Merrell Inn, an historic lodge in Stockbridge, Massachusettes. I returned to my maiden name and within a couple of years became the fulltime theater reviewer under my new byline.

Unfortunately, many people, even copy editors at The Press, insist on misspelling my last name as Merrill. I try to tell them,

"M-E-R-R-E-L-L, the same as the shoes," figuring they might misspell a writer's name but not an advertiser.

Damn Yankee

About 50 journalists crowded into a narrow conference room in a downtown Pittsburgh hotel that morning in May 1996. They were setting up cameras and shaking hands. I felt a little left out because I didn't know a soul. I made a game of trying to guess by dress and demeanor which ones were on-screen personalities versus the less flashy representatives from small publications or radio stations. I was seated in the middle of the room, but I was surveying the people sitting behind me when a face peeked through the curtain at the rear wall. It was the man we had come to see—comedy icon Jerry Lewis. He giggled mischievously when he realized a few of us had spotted him checking out  the crowd. A few minutes later he strode through the door at the front of the room, surrounded by his entourage.

Lewis and his handsome partner, Dean Martin, were famous entertainers before I was born, and I was only eight by the time they split in 1956. To me, Jerry Lewis was "The Nutty Professor" or any one of the dozens of other rubber-faced clowns in his 60 films. The press conference was for a tour of the Broadway show "Damn Yankees" in which Lewis portrayed the devil.

Broadway tours usually don't have press conferences. Print media, radio and television usually set up individual interviews. But Lewis, who was 70 at the time, was a star of such stature that the media gladly lined up to take their best shot at what is known affectionately as a group grope.

Lewis refused to do advance phone interviews, so the only way The Grand Rapids Press could get a story into the paper before the tour came to town was to send a reporter to one of the cities where the tour would stop prior to Grand Rapids. This was back in the days of economic boom, when The Press still had a travel budget. I was assistant features editor then, responsible for assigning someone to the task. David Nicolette, our longtime theater reporter, was not interested in traveling across the country just to talk to some uppity comedian who wouldn't do a phone interview. The tour schedule put "Damn Yankees" in Pittsburgh a few weeks before Grand Rapids and my son, Ryan, was attending the Art Institute of Pittsburgh, within walking distance of the hotel where Lewis would be staying. It didn't take me long to decide who to send.

At the Pittsburgh press conference, Lewis was the playful entertainer the journalists wanted to see. He was traveling with his wife and 4-year-old daughter and elaborately described all they had to carry.

"When we arrive at the airport, we look like the Joads from "Grapes of Wrath," he said.

He also responded to questions with witty one-liners.

Q. What haven't you done that you would like to do?

A. I've always wanted to be a Viking.

Q. What took you so long to make it to Broadway?

A. I had a flat.

At the end of the allotted hour, he posed for photographs with starstruck reporters.

I suppose this is as good a time as any to interject that I never posed for photos with the stars I interviewed and I never asked for autographs. First, there's the practical reason that such trophies end up stuck in a drawer somewhere and never displayed anyway. But more important, I think it turns the reporter into a fan. It undermines the position of professional journalist. I respected the artists I interviewed for the work they did and I expected them to respect my work as well.

I hung around the back of the room while Lewis posed for photographs. Then I got into an elevator with Lewis, his publicist and another gentleman and went to his suite for a private interview. After all, I had flown several hundred miles, so we wanted a story that would go beyond the press-conference quotes everyone would see on the wire the next day.

I was impressed with how fit and trim Lewis was at 70. He looked nice in jeans and a sweater. The hotel suite had a big dining table and a living room. Lewis took a seat on the sofa and I sat in a nearby chair with my tape recorder on the table between us. I don't usually record interviews—it takes a lot of time to transcribe—but I didn't want to miss anything.

I had read everything I could get my hands on in preparation for the interview, so I tried to steer the conversation to topics that hadn't been explored before, such as his one previous visit to Grand Rapids in 1949 to talk to potential donors for the fight against muscular dystrophy. We chatted a lot about his daughter, one of his favorite topics, and he entertained me with an impromptu impersonation of George Burns.

The publicist had told me not to ask about Dean Martin, who had died a few months before the interview. But I knew their partnership would be of interest to my readers. So, I asked all my other questions and when, after about 15 minutes, the publicist told me to wrap it up, I asked about Dean Martin. If Lewis refused to answer and kicked me out, I already had enough for a story.

But Lewis answered me graciously, even though he awkwardly used the phrase "my partner" instead of Martin's name.

"What we had will never be seen again in the history of show business," he told me. "What we had was a kind of magic that's impossible to define. It had nothing to do with the talent process. It had to do with the love of two men. Losing him was like losing a limb."

My story ran on the cover of the Entertainment section the following Sunday. A few days later, when the tour opened in Grand Rapids, there was another press conference. I attended out of courtesy and respect for this comedic talent, even though we did not plan to write another story.

The meeting room at the Amway Grand Plaza Hotel was abuzz with cameras being set up and media competitors chatting over the spread of morning snacks. It was a smaller crowd than in Pittsburgh, with a couple of television stations represented, a couple of radio stations and a few out-of-town papers. The most familiar face in the room was retail magnate Fred Meijer, whose company was sponsoring the tour's appearance in Grand Rapids. Meijer was flitting around the room like a firefly lighting sparks of goodwill among the just-another-day journalists. He passed out coupons for a free Purple Cow ice cream at one of his stores and greeted television personality or hotel waitress with the same enthusiasm.

I was seated in the front row when Lewis came in to address the group of 10 or so. He recognized me immediately as the reporter who had interviewed him a week earlier and said he had seen my story.

"You write pretty well—for a woman," he quipped.

"You're pretty funny—for a man," I wanted to reply, but I just smiled. I didn't take it personally. I knew he was trying to be funny, but no one laughed.

A couple of reporters asked questions and Lewis made some snide remark about a cameraman from one of the television stations who was asking his own questions. Less than five minutes into the press conference, one of the television reporters asked if Lewis ever tires of all the touring and telethons.

"What makes me tired is when I'm in a place I shouldn't be, like here," he snapped. "There are more people in my suite."

With that, he thanked everyone for coming and rushed out of the room, his entourage scurrying behind.

I wanted to stand up and scold him. I thought maybe I was supposed to be the character in "The Nutty Professor" who calls him on his self-centeredness and makes him turn around and transform back into his kinder, funnier self. But this wasn't a movie and he didn't turn around. His rude outburst ran on the local television stations and radio stations. Longtime fans were insulted and angry.

Jerry Lewis may be a funny man, but he didn't always leave them laughing.

Reach Out and Touch Someone

Most of my interviews with stars were via the telephone. Phones took me into bedrooms in Los Angeles, rehearsal halls in New York City and even the misty hills of Ireland. I woke up a groggy David Copperfield in Las Vegas. I found 74-year-old Debbie Reynolds a little hoarse at her California home after three nights of performing in Reno. Maurice Hines was on a Christmas break from the Broadway tour of "Guys and Dolls" and about to go holiday shopping with his daughter in New York.

"Prairie Home Companion's" Garrison Keillor interrupted the interview to answer the front door at his Minnesota home. His wife had been shopping and was locked out. I had a hard time coaxing anything more than a yes or no answer from crooner Andy Williams, but Bobby Vinton was so enthusiastic, I couldn't write fast enough.

Most of the time, the stars I interviewed were on tour with a Broadway show or a concert, so I was given a hotel to call. Most were listed under their own names at the reception desk, but some, like the late Eartha Kitt, used a pseudonym to ensure privacy.

Kitt was touring as the fairy godmother in "Cinderella." She answered the phone midsentence in a conversation with her daughter/manager, Kitt Shapiro. Then without formalities, she turned her attention to the phone. "It's me," she said with a laugh, and then told her grandchildren to turn down the television. It's that kind of disarming informality that made phone interviews fun.

After the tour arrived in Grand Rapids, I got the opportunity to interview the 73-year-old Kitt again, in person. I was working on a story about diversity on stage, and I thought her perspective after 55 years in theater would help.

"Theater has no race," she told me between television interviews. "Legitimate theater has always been the one place where you could find talented people without regard to race."

The Cinderella tour, for instance, made no apologies or explanation for its multiracial royal family with a black actor portraying the king, a white actress playing the queen and an Asian in the role of the prince. Theater has more freedom than movies or television, she told me, because those media are more commercial.

"They're afraid if you see a face you don't like, you won't buy the product," she said.

Sometimes performers stack up a whole day of interviews before they head out on a tour. I remember talking to Jay Leno in 1988, when he was a regular Monday night guest host on the Tonight Show. His upcoming visit to Joliet was part of a standup comedy tour. Our talk was one of 17 interviews he had scheduled back-to-back that day. You can't expect much spontaneity with such an interview production line.

Leno spoke to me from one of the two garages in his Hollywood Hills home, the one with 18 motorcycles, he told me. The problem with interviewing a comedian is the interviewer wants to play straight man and have the comedian respond with a punch line. It doesn't work that way.

I mentioned that several writers had described Leno's prominent chin as "anvil face," "Pelican chin" or "Dudley Do-right." I expected him to have a quip or two of his own, but he wasn't playing that game.

"When you make fun of yourself you give other people license to do the same," he said. "It's bound to get to you after a while. These looks aren't so bad. I've gotten laid lots of times with these looks."

Cell phones liberated interviews. I talked to Broadway choreographer/director Jerry Mitchell while he was walking his dog in Central Park. Cherry Jones, the Tony Award-winning star of Broadway's "Doubt," was walking down the sidewalk in Manhattan and bumped into a friend she hadn't seen in a while so she interrupted the interview for a short chat. Tony Award-winning Broadway actor Greg Jbara paused the interview to go through the checkout line in a store.

Cell phones also turned interviews into dropped-call nightmares. Just when a star was in the middle of a great quote, the signal would go away. If the subject was aboard a tour bus going through the mountains, an interview could be interrupted a half-dozen times.

I always tried to do my interviews from a landline to reduce the number of cell phones involved. But sometimes I had no choice. I interviewed Bernadette Peters a couple of times. Once, the PR person misunderstood and scheduled the interview on a day when I was driving back from a holiday weekend. I accepted the appointment anyway and gave the PR person my cell phone number. I pulled off the road about 15 minutes before the interview was scheduled and sat in a parking lot at Wendy's waiting for my phone to ring.

Peters was coming to Grand Rapids to sing with the Grand Rapids Symphony. I got the assignment because I had interviewed her before when she appeared on Broadway in "Annie Get Your Gun" with Tom Wopat, a local favorite. She also had played Mama Rose in "Gypsy" with West Michigan actress Kate Reinders portraying her daughter, Dainty June. Peters and I had lots of good conversations. We even shared hair pointers, since we both have naturally curly red hair (the curl is natural; the red not so much.)

At the time of my Wendy's parking lot interview, Peters was about to publish her first children's book—a story based on her dog, Kramer. One of the songs she was going to sing in Grand Rapids was a lullaby she had written for the book. Peters is a great animal lover, and the book, "Broadway Barks," was raising money for the charity she had started with the same name.

We had a lovely visit, chatting about her dogs and her book and writing her first song. It was the kind of conversation that would have been right at home sitting down at a table in that fast food restaurant. I thought about that as I watched customers coming and going during our conversation. If the elegant redhead had been sitting with me in the car, she would have attracted attention, I'm sure. But passersby had no idea I was talking with a Tony Award-winning Broadway actress, comedienne and movie star.

One afternoon I was in the middle of writing a story when my office phone rang. "This is Marvin Hamlisch," the voice said.

I had been trying to set up an interview with Hamlisch, who was coming to town for the reopening of the Grand Rapids Civic Theatre after a $10 million restoration. I hadn't heard back from the PR person to set up an interview time, but Hamlisch was sitting in an airport in San Francisco, waiting for a plane. He took a chance and called. I was glad to hear from him but spent a minute or two shuffling through my desk to clear the project I had been working on and find a clean yellow legal pad and working pen.

I usually transcribed phone interviews on a yellow legal pad, in-person interviews on a narrow reporter's notebook. Younger reporters usually take notes directly into the computer, but I've never developed that skill. My typing was too slow and I was constantly interrupting myself to correct typos. My handwritten scrawl was quicker and I was more able to catch every word when an interviewee was on a roll with a great quote. Besides, I think the sound of a keyboard clacking can be disruptive to the subject.

My interview with Hamlisch focused on "A Chorus Line," one of the longest running shows on Broadway. A revival was opening on Broadway a month after our interview and a few days later Civic would open its production of "A Chorus Line." Hamlisch was talking to me from San Francisco, where he had just finished recording the cast album for the revival.

"I have a lot of pride in this show," he told me. "I knew it was special but I didn't know it would run 15 years. I think it is great that it will talk to a whole new generation."

In preparing for the interview, I read about "The Overture That Never Was," a number Hamlisch wrote for the show that was never used. When I mentioned my discovery to Penelope Notter, who was directing Civic's production of "A Chorus Line," she said that would be the perfect piece for Hamlisch to play at the reopening gala. Like most overtures, it incorporates bits and pieces of all the songs in the show, and turned out to be ideal for the event.

Sometimes, even with all the means of communication at our disposal, it was hard to make connections. In 2004, Bette Midler brought her 40-city "Kiss My Brass" tour to Grand Rapids' Van Andel Arena. I set up an interview for a few weeks before the event. I was supposed to receive a call from her at 11 a.m., but a few minutes before the interview was scheduled, the PR person called to see if she could reschedule for noon. Then noon came, 12:15, 12:20. I called the PR person. She apologized and said she would check into it. Meanwhile, I was sitting at the desk, afraid to leave for lunch or start another project for fear I would miss the call.

An hour or so later, the PR person called back. The interview was rescheduled for 3 p.m. By 3:10 I was on the phone to the agent again. She promised 4 p.m., then called me back and said, "How about 5 p.m.?" When the phone didn't ring by 5:05, I called the PR person again. I could imagine sitting at that desk all night. I told the PR person I was leaving for home and would be there by 5:30. I didn't want to use my cell phone, so I gave her my son's landline. Then I rushed home and barged into my son's apartment.

"Don't answer your phone if it rings," I told him. "I'm expecting a call from Bette Midler. It's been a very bad day."

"Bette Midler is calling you at home and that's your idea of a bad day?" my son said dumfounded.

Finally the phone rang at about 6 p.m. Unfortunately, the PR person stayed on the line and the three-way connection caused a lot of interference. I could barely hear what the normally energetic singer had to say. Midler seemed impatient with the whole interview idea, angry with me before I asked the first question. She never apologized for all the delays or made any explanation. She said touring was difficult and she was tired.

"It's very hard to do. My schedule's not as hard as some but it's still hard," she said in a whiny pout. " I'm not getting any fresh air."

She answered a few questions, but the PR person ended the call after exactly six minutes. From this, I had to write the lead story for that Sunday's Entertainment section. And I had to stifle my anger at being jerked around all day.

Now you might think I could turn this into some expose on a star's bad behavior, but the truth is, doing interviews isn't Bette Midler's job. Her job is to entertain and she does it very well. She was going to fill that arena with or without an interview in The Grand Rapids Press. Did she owe her fans a few comments in the local paper? We'd like to think so. But she didn't have to be nice about it. I had the difficult task of writing an objective story worthy of the event, untainted by personal feelings. It would have been childish for me to put her down in the story or complain about her treatment of the media.   The reader didn't care about my bad day.

 In addition to the six quotes I gleaned from the short interview, I filled in with background about the tour and tidbits on her career that I'd found in my research. The resulting story was a good read, worthy of the lead position, with only that one "fresh air" comment giving any inkling of the tired, whiny woman I had interviewed.

Less than a week later, I reviewed her performance, which was simply divine. She mentioned a couple of times that she was tired, and made huffing and puffing part of her shtick. It was an entertaining, uplifting evening, and I said so in the review. If she was having a bad day, she didn't let it show.

Former Idols

Ever notice how the big stars of our youth seem to keep on shining in our eyes long after their careers have crashed like meteorites?

I mean, I remember the day in 1959 when I read about Eddie Fisher leaving Debbie Reynolds for Elizabeth Taylor. I was only 11 but I was getting my annual perm, sitting in a beauty shop under one of those bouffant hair dryers. Debbie Reynolds and Liz Taylor were like gods to me. I couldn't foresee that they wouldn't always be the most famous people on the planet.

Fifty years later, when Brad Pitt left Jennifer Aniston for Angelina Jolie, I could see some comparisons, but in my mind, the current star gossip always would be trivial in a way that Debbie, Liz, and Eddie never could be.

Of all the movies and television shows Reynolds did, my favorite was 1957's "Tammy and the Bachelor." Tammy's wide-eyed innocence has always been my idea of feminine perfection, and Reynolds singing "Tammy's In Love" in three-quarter time runs through my mind at the very mention of the name.

Reynolds, however, probably has a lot more in common with her spunky title role in the 1964 movie "The Unsinkable Molly Brown." At age 74, when I interviewed her in 2006, she still was performing 42 weeks a year. And the one-woman cabaret she brought to Grand Rapids was lively and fun.

Her greatest source of pride, she told me, was not one of her many movies but her two children, actress Carrie Fisher and son Todd Fisher. Her life's ambition is to build a Hollywood museum—for which she has accumulated an extensive collection of memorabilia—but she keeps running into financial snags.

"American film has influenced the world," she said. "Why shouldn't we preserve our history? We have museums for airplanes and bowling and everything else."

I know it's a factor of my age that I'm much more interested in talking to a "has-been" like Debbie Reynolds than wannabes such as all the "American Idol" contestants who show up in Broadway tours. When "Joseph and the Amazing Technicolor Dreamcoat" came to town in 2006 with Patrick Cassidy and "American Idol" finalist Amy Adams, I wanted to interview Cassidy, who's at least the son of somebody I consider famous (Shirley Jones and Jack Cassidy). There are enough Cassidy stars in that family, including David, Shaun and Ryan Cassidy, to create their own fantasy basketball team.

Patrick told a great story about the filming of "The Music Man" in 1961, when his mother, who portrayed Marian the librarian, was pregnant with him. In the scene where Marian and Harold Hill (Robert Preston) embrace on the footbridge, Patrick made his presence known by kicking Preston. Almost 20 years later, Patrick and Robert Preston were doing a benefit together. When Patrick introduced himself, Preston said "We've already met."

I'm sorry, no American Idol can tell a story like that.

But, of course, my editor, John Gonzalez, insisted I interview Amy Adams, too. I have to admit the bulk of today's younger readers—who never saw "The Music Man" and don't know who Robert Preston was—were certainly more interested in Amy Adams. Her best story was about the surprise call when she was offered the role of narrator in "Joseph and the Amazing Technicolor Dreamcoat."

"I was seven months pregnant, lying on the couch eating bon bons, and some stranger calls. It was that out of the blue, " she told me.

Adams also turned out to be quite talented in the show, and was very personable when the cast toured a pediatric ward at Spectrum Medical Center in Grand Rapids. But a nice personality, a good singing voice and a couple of appearances on a television talent show don't constitute a star in my eyes.

Mighty Mickey

Perhaps the biggest movie icon I interviewed was the pint-sized comedian Mickey Rooney.

The impish actor has been performing almost all of the 90 years of his life. Born into a vaudeville family, he was named Joe Yule Jr. but legally changed his name to Mickey after he starred as Mickey McGuire in a series of short films when he was 7 years old. Most people know him as Andy Hardy, the character he played opposite Judy Garland, in 15 films from 1937-1946. He continued in movies such as "National Velvet," did some stage work ("Sugar Babies), won an Emmy for his television role, "Bill," and even appeared in the 2006 film "A Night in the Museum."

"I made some good ones and some bad ones," Rooney told me when I asked about his movie resume. "I've made pictures that were so bad they weren't released. They escaped."

I first covered Rooney in Joliet in 1989, when he was doing a comedy tour with dancer and actor Donald O'Connor. The performance fell on Rooney's 69th birthday, so the Rialto Square Theatre, an elaborate palace-like facility, planned a surprise birthday party. At the curtain call, silver and burgundy balloons rained down and somebody wheeled in a cake. The onstage band started playing "Happy Birthday," and the applauding audience sang along.

The 5-foot-3-inch Rooney seemed flustered. It wasn't the happy response we were expecting. If anything, he seemed irritated. I guess he didn't like surprises.

He quickly took charge of the situation and turned the spotlight on his co-star, O'Connor, whose birthday had been about a month earlier. He led the audience in another chorus of "Happy Birthday" for O'Connor.

But the Rialto staffers weren't finished with surprises. They brought out a handmade card featuring a sketch of Rooney in his much younger days.

"There's my hair," the balding entertainer exclaimed.

The whole celebration seemed awkward, however. Rooney wasn't in a party mood. Maybe he was tired after his performance. Maybe he had other celebration plans. Maybe he just didn't want to be reminded he was a year older. But he clearly wanted to get this celebration over as quickly as possible.

The curtains closed; the audience left.

O'Connor stuck around to party backstage with a small group of Rialto supporters, but Rooney declined and quickly disappeared.

It was much different in 2002, when Rooney and his eighth wife, Jan Chamberlain, brought an evening of music and comedy to Grand Rapids' Wealthy Theatre. After their 80-minute show, the couple seemed to have all the time in the world to stay in the lobby signing CDs.

Although Rooney still had plenty of spunk, the 13 years between the two shows had worn on his voice, which was about as

thin as his wispy white hair. His wife sang some bluesy solos and Patsy Cline songs, as well as duets with Rooney.

I recognized some of the comedy bits in the Wealthy Theatre show that seemed recycled from the Rialto show, such as a Jimmy Durante impersonation. But the 300 people in the Wealthy Theater audience were about a fifth the size of the crowd a few years earlier at the Rialto. Not only was Rooney getting older, but also the fans who loved him in the '30s and '40s were dying out.

I couldn't help but think how sad it was that a man who had made more than 100 movies was spending his declining years begging for an audience in an old restored movie theater. It was hard to imagine that this little man had charmed sex goddess Ava Gardner as his first wife in 1942, back when he was the biggest box-office draw for three years running.

But Rooney was philosophical about his turn of fortune – and his string of divorces.

"You know what alimony is? It's pumping gas into another guy's car," he quipped. "I've pumped a lot of gas."

May the Force Be with You

Manistee's Ramsdell Theatre erupted with applause when favorite son James Earl Jones strode onto the stage that August day in 2003. With a shy, toothy grin, the hulking, 6-foot, 2-inch actor promptly sat in small, red velvet Victorian chair that looked too delicate to hold such a big man. This was the stage where the award-winning actor had cut his acting teeth half a century ago. He seemed to feel so at home that while he waited to take the podium for the morning press conference, he stretched out and leaned the chair back on two legs like a gangly teenager, balancing his bulk on spindly pieces of wood only slightly bigger around than his thumb.

I could imagine a mother somewhere scolding him to "sit right," but Jones has defied more than gravity in his life.

Born in Mississippi, he grew up in rural northern Michigan and often returned to the state where he graduated from high school, started his acting career and still has relatives. Jones is known for a variety of roles, from Alex Haley on television's famed miniseries "Roots: The Next Generation" to the voice of

Darth Vader in the original "Star Wars" trilogy and the voice of Mufasa in the animated movie "The Lion King."

I was privileged to cover several of his visits to Michigan, but two encounters are especially memorable, because they were about as challenging as his balancing act on the antique chair.

Actually, Jones had nothing to do with the problems I had at our first meeting at that Manistee press conference in 2003. The theater was presenting "An Evening with James Earl Jones" as part of its centennial celebration. The media were invited to a morning press conference but weren't allowed to cover the sold-out performance that evening. From a news point of view, the press conference is only half the story, and we needed to tell our readers about the performance as well.

But when I headed up to Manistee that morning, my editors seemed satisfied with the access we had been granted. I was to return to Grand Rapids in the afternoon to write the story for the next day's paper. There was no plan for me to get a room and set up a computer to send from there, which would be the only practical way to cover a morning press conference and an evening performance.

Shortly after I arrived, however, I received a call that the plan had changed. I was to find some way to get into that performance. Never mind that there wasn't space to report on both events or that my workday already was being stretched to the max just to drive more than two hours each way, cover the conference and write the story. If I stayed for the performance, drove back and wrote the story, I'd be working about 20 hours straight.

But I didn't have time to worry about that. I had a press conference to cover. "I didn't plan to become an actor when I came here," Jones told the reporters. "The prospect was like going to the moon."

He started as a carpenter at Ramsdell and was happy to build sets until the theater decided to do "Othello" and Jones was cast as the dark-skinned Moor.

"The people of Manistee must have had a lot of faith in me, or they were ready for a trip to the moon," he said.

Needless to say, Jones charmed us for about an hour with more stories than I ever could fit into the allotted space.

After the press conference, I sought out Civic Players executive director Ron Steinberg. If anyone could get me into that performance, I figured he could. He had taken me on a tour of the facility about a year earlier when I did a story on the building's restoration, so I knew where his office was. I went through the public display area and opened an unmarked door at the back. I knew it opened into the backstage area, which also led to the director's office.

I burst through the door and smack-dab into James Earl Jones, who was quietly talking with some dignitaries. If I had been seeking a one-on-one interview, I might have been successful, but I was more interested in assuring the startled star that I was not trying to ambush him, only to obtain access to his performance.

I quickly found Steinberg and pulled him away from the others. I explained my boss's insistence that I cover the performance and told him I'd be more than happy to stand in the rear of the auditorium or accept any limited-view spot that might be available. Again I was told it would be impossible.

I hung around the building trying to spot a hiding place where I could await the evening's production but was ushered outside as the building was closed. Hanging around outside, I ran into Paul and Maureen Dreher of Grand Rapids. Paul, who had been managing director of Grand Rapids Civic Theatre for 39 years before retiring, had been part of the theater company at Ramsdell in his youth and had roomed with Jones. The Drehers had tickets for that evening's performance and were meeting other friends there, but I couldn't' convince any of them to sell one of their tickets to me.

As we talked about Paul's history with the theater, he decided to take me in through the backstage door—which was unlocked—and show me around backstage as he told stories of those days. Again, I was contemplating finding a hiding place inside the theater —even though the idea of a possible confrontation frightened me.

Instead, I hit upon another idea. I asked Paul to be my eyes inside the theater. He agreed to call me after the performance and tell me how it went. I would head back to Grand Rapids and write the highlights of the press conference to be topped with Paul's comments on the performance. The best of both worlds.

The plan worked well, although it was 11 p.m. by the time I got Paul's comments. Jones presented a program he called "Shakespeare in the Minority Key," with readings from "The Merchant of Venice," "Titus Andronicus" and, of course, "Othello."

"It was more like a conversation than a performance," Dreher said. "It felt like déjà vu when he was reading from 'Othello.'"

Two years later, Jones returned to the Ramsdell for an event to raise money for a community center in nearby Brethren, the rural town where he graduated from high school in 1949. The school held a special spot in Jones' memory. He had a severe stuttering problem as a boy. Donald Crouch, one of the teachers at Brethren High School, helped him overcome his affliction by having him read poetry to the class. The cadence of the poetry and the act of reading instead of "speaking" gave Jones the vocal control he needed and unleashed one of the greatest voices of stage and film.

"I want to help put a roof on that old building," Jones said in a phone interview from his home in upstate New York. "That building is the route through which I entered into the career I'm in now. Because of that school, I entered the world of words."

The school had helped arrange the phone interview, and Jones was quite gracious with his time, but at a couple of points during the conversation, my questions hit a nerve and I found myself shivering under the booming rebuke of Darth Vader.

The first snag came when I asked about his 2004 appearance in "On Golden Pond" on Broadway. Jones has a long stage history, including winning a Tony Award for "The Great White Hope" in 1969. But the run of "On Golden Pond," his most recent show, was cut short when Jones became ill.

Usually, it takes more than a star's illness to cancel a successful play. Capable understudies have replaced lots of big name stars. I suspected there was more behind the cancellation, but I didn't have any preconceived notion what that might be. Maybe Jones was more seriously ill than the papers had reported, or the play had other problems and illness was a convenient excuse, or maybe Jones was just tired of the show. I brought up the subject to see if Jones might shed a little light on why the show closed early. If nothing else, it was a great opportunity for him to brag that the show couldn't go on without him. When he didn't say anything, I added an off-hand comment like, "so you're all better now?" or something like that, and Jones took my suggestion way too seriously.

"It was just a cold. Of course I'm better. Why wouldn't I be better? It wasn't cancer. Did you think it was cancer? Who said it was cancer?"

I was shocked at his angry reaction. I stumbled around—probably stuttering a bit myself—and managed to smooth that over and get a few more interesting comments before I fell off the brink again. I mentioned I had seen "The 25th Annual Putnam County Spelling Bee" in Chicago and one of the actors was named James Earl Jones II. I knew Jones had a son about that age, but I thought his name was Flynn, so I asked if this young actor might be some other relative or perhaps another son.

Jones exploded. I don't know whether he was angry with me for bringing it up or just angry that an actor dared to use his name and fame. "There are rules against that," he said in a booming voice, and railed on for another minute or so at top volume.

I was so upset by his reactions to such innocuous questions that my hands were shaking. I had enough comments for my story so I quickly thanked him and brought the interview to a close. To my surprise, Jones turned suddenly quiet and thanked me for my time. I can't tell you how rare that is for an actor to thank a reporter. He seemed so kind that I immediately wondered if I had misinterpreted what I thought was an angry outburst.

After I hung up, I replayed the conversation through my mind. Had he just been teasing and I misunderstood? Or had he really been that angry? Later that evening, I ran into Paul Dreher at an event I was covering. I told him about my interview and asked if he had ever known Jones to have a problem with his temper.

"I think he's just more intelligent than most people," Dreher suggested. "He anticipates where a line of questioning may be going. He's always a step ahead."

Was that it? Were my questions too personal? Was I approaching subjects that were more sensitive than I knew?

A few weeks later, I covered the fundraiser and enjoyed Jones' reading for the packed theater. Many of the people who lined up outside the theater had gone to school with Jones and called him Todd, his childhood nickname. To them, Jones wasn't just a local boy who became famous. He was a star who was kind-hearted enough to come back and help raise money for a community center in a town so small it isn't on most maps.

"It really brought back memories for me," said Marvin Lagerquist, who was two years behind Jones at Brethren High School. "(Teacher Donald) Crouch told him if he didn't get that slush out of his mouth, he wasn't going to go anywhere."

In Jones' performance, there was no trace of the temper I had encountered on the phone. Even during the question-and-answer period, when an obstinate man in the audience insisted on pursuing political questions, Jones remained calmly in charge.

"I listen to a lot of politics," he said diplomatically, "and I don't hear much."

Michigan Maid

In addition to James Earl Jones, several other actors with Michigan connections were practically on my speed dial. I know Kim Zimmer felt that way. Zimmer, who played Reva Shayne Lewis on "Guiding Light" for more than 25 years, grew up just outside Grand Rapids. Whenever Daytime Emmy nominations came around, I would give her a call to see if she thought she'd get a nomination and then call her back if she got a nomination and then call her back again if she won. And to make matters worse, I also did interviews when she returned to the area to appear at a fund raiser or perform at the Augusta Barn Theatre, a professional summer stock theater about 40 miles south of Grand Rapids.

In 2006, when she was performing at The Barn as Mama Rose in "Gypsy," we decided to do an in-depth profile, which meant I talked with her sister, daughter and "Guiding Light" co-star, Robert Newman, in addition to conducting an hour-long in-person interview with Zimmer and observing rehearsal for another hour. I wanted to get a comment from her husband, director A.C. Weary, and happened to spot him and their sons, Max and Jake, at the opening night performance of "Gypsy." Trying to catch them in the parking lot, however, I tripped over a curb and went flying onto the hood of a parked car. I think I scared Jake to death and convinced him paparazzi are alive and well in West Michigan.

We also wanted a good display of photos to go with the story, a family album of sorts, including a baby picture of the actress. Neither Zimmer nor her sister Karen had the photos I needed, so I called her elderly parents in Florida, who were completely confused by my request for a baby picture of their famous daughter. Considering my own aging parents, I could understand. It is not the sort of thing people have at their fingertips, certainly not after packing up everything and moving into a condo.

I was about to give up entirely when I got the idea to check a photo file created by my predecessor, David Nicolette. Dave's file was created in the days when every release came with black-and-white glossies, cameras still had film and digital meant a clock with numbers instead of hands. To my surprise, I found dozens of photos of Zimmer in Dave's file, including a preschool photo that even the actress didn't remember.

In the profile interview, Zimmer and I discussed details that never had come up in all our quick interviews, such as the way Zimmer met her husband when they were both interns at Hope Summer Repertory Theatre. Zimmer played the fairy queen Titiana, who falls in love with Bottom, a half-donkey man played by A.C. Weary.

"He was the most talented person I'd ever met," Zimmer said. "He could juggle and fence and sing and dance and act. He had the ability to enchant. I felt when I met him he was someone I was going to be with the rest of my life."

Her feelings were pretty accurate. By the time "Guiding Light" was canceled in 2009, Zimmer's character had been married so many times even the soap magazines got confused. But in real life, Zimmer and Weary had been together 28 years and raised three children.

"You've got to be on the same side when you put your head on the pillow," Zimmer told me. "Some nights we giggle before we go to bed at how ridiculous we have been during the day."

More than anything, the profile revealed that Zimmer was very much like the fans who are addicted to "Guiding Light." Until she hired a cleaning company a few years ago, she had done all the housekeeping and laundry for the family. "I go to the grocery store, take the car to be worked on, take the garbage to the street," she told me.

She also took a commuter bus and subway from her New Jersey home into Manhattan.

"If people recognize me, they think it's cool that I take the bus," she said. "When you're walking through the hot tunnels of the subway station with a throng of people, you're all sweating together."

Look Around You

I interviewed my first Michigan celebrity long before moving to the state. I was working in Charleston, South Carolina, in 1974 when Grand Rapids' favorite son, Gerald R. Ford, became president. The editors discovered that his brother, Tom, a member of the Michigan State Legislature, had a place on Seabrook Island near Charleston. I was sent to do a lifestyle piece on this branch of the presidential family.

It was my first time dealing with the Secret Service, which is like airline security on steroids. Do NOT try to crack a joke. These guys imagine communists and terrorists under every bed. I guess they have to. But when the News & Courier wanted to do a story on Tom Ford's little condo on the golf course, we were forbidden to shoot any photos of the condo, inside or out. Might give away the layout, they said, make the family vulnerable. Of course, every condo in the development has the same layout, so any enterprising bad guy could have gotten as many details as he wanted by visiting another unit.

But, hey, in an effort to get along and get the story, we planned a picnic on the golf course, which actually ended up posed in a sprawling old oak tree with branches curling along the ground at perfect table height. We also took photos of Tom Ford, his wife, daughter and son-in-law in their golf cart. Although we couldn't photograph the condo, I was allowed to visit there and the family was just jumping with excitement to show me their most recent purchase – a color television. It tickled me to think the same material things that excite most folks excited the brother of the most powerful man in the world.

Tom Wopat—Luke from the original "Dukes of Hazzard"—is an honorary Michigander, even though he grew up on a Wisconsin dairy farm. Before he was hot-rodding through American living rooms, he was at Augusta's Barn Theatre earning his membership in Equity, the professional actor's union. He returns there frequently to do shows.

I like Wopat because he's so down-to-earth. In 2004, Wopat was scheduled to play Sky Masterson in "Guys and Dolls" at The Barn. A few weeks before, I caught up with him on the New Jersey Turnpike. He was returning a rental car to pick up his truck, which had been in the shop for a new transmission, and he interrupted the interview to thank the toll-booth operator. Another time I called, he was in the middle of laying the brick for a patio at his New Jersey home. When he was on tour as Billy Flynn in "Chicago" he told me he liked to get a room with a kitchen and fix a pot of chili or roast a chicken.

"I prefer homemade food to going out to eat," he told me. "I go out often enough when I have to. If I get a choice, I'd rather eat in."

I've always been amazed when talking to Wopat that he has so many irons in the fire. He'll take a break from a show on Broadway, such as "Chicago," to come to Michigan for a couple of weeks to do "Guys and Dolls" and then leave before the run is over for a new musical at the Williamstown Theatre Festival in Massachusetts. He reminds me of those carpenters who always juggle six jobs at once, making a morning appearance at one, a lunchtime stop at another and finishing the day someplace else, trying to keep everybody happy.

And Wopat succeeds. He was nominated for a Tony Award in 1999 for his portrayal of Frank Butler in "Annie Get Your Gun." In 2004, he won a Drama Desk Award as part of the ensemble of "Glengarry Glen Ross" and portrayed Julian Marsh in "42nd Street" in 2002-03. That's not including six country music albums, two jazz albums, films such as 1998's "Meteorites!" and television appearances such as his recurring role on "Cybill" in 1995.

I also caught best-selling Michigan author Mitch Albom on the road, but it was much different from Wopat's casual conversation with the toll-booth operator. A Detroit Free-Press sports writer, Albom catapulted to national fame with his best-selling book "Tuesdays With Morrie." I first talked with him when his play, "Duck Hunter Shoots Angel," was being produced by a local theater. Albom is as busy as Wopat, so he told me he usually scheduled interviews for the travel time between The Free-Press and his ESPN television show. But he has a driver navigating the tollbooths and traffic while he conducts interviews from his back-seat office.

Although I've never had a chance to interview Michigan's most famous performer—Madonna—I did do a story on Ciccone Vineyard and Winery, the northern Michigan winery owned by her father, Silvio "Tony" Ciccone. High atop a hill overlooking West Grand Traverse Bay, the site is beyond picturesque, but very much a family project. The day I visited about 10 years ago, Madonna's youngest brother, Mario, was visiting from Los Angeles to help with the opening of a tasting room on the property.

His stepmother, Joan, gave me a tour of the vineyards while we waited for Ciccone to return from a shopping trip. About 20 minutes after our appointed meeting time, Ciccone pulled up in a pick-up truck loaded with lumber.

"Never go to Home Depot on a Saturday," he said, offering a handshake.

Ciccone made it clear when I arranged the interview that he would talk about his wine but not about his daughter. He was wary, and I was honestly there to do a story about the winery. But, of course, the fame of the winemaker's daughter was part of the reason we wanted to do the story, so I had to win his trust, put him at ease talking about his winery, and then cautiously feed in a few questions about the Material Girl.

"She has her life and we're doing our thing," he said, adding he didn't think her fame would attract visitors to the winery.

"I think they will come because they like wine," he said.

Madonna plugged Papa's wine on the Rosie O'Donnell television show, Ciccone said with a proud smile, but you won't find her photo on the label. Though he talks wine lingo, using words like "bouquet" and "bite" as he pours samples into wine glasses, Ciccone looks like any farmer in jeans and a flannel shirt.

"Believe me, it's a lot of work ," he said. "Physical work." He described recontouring the land, clearing vegetation, planting vineyards – much of which was done by him, his wife and grown children. The son of Italian immigrants, Ciccone learned winemaking from his father but didn't get into the business until he retired from a career as an engineer for Chrysler in Detroit. The secret of good wine, he said, is in the grape. "If it's not there, no matter what you do, you can't make it better," he said.

As for Michael Moore and me, I met Michigan's controversial documentary director at a writers' conference on Walloon Lake. His wife, Kathleen Glynn, was one of the organizers of the conference, so I got to see Moore as a fellow creative soul and not so much as the loudmouth liberal who tried to chase down Roger Smith, the former CEO of General Motors, in his debut documentary "Roger & Me."

When Moore spoke to the group about his writing and his movies, everything he said was outrageously opinionated and usually entertaining. But he also stood in the buffet line with us and jockeyed for position in a group photo on the last day of the three-day conference. In the on-site bookstore, he came up to me and recommended Julia Cameron's "The Right to Write," and it has always been my favorite book on writing.

I returned to that conference four years in a row and grew to admire Moore as a regular guy who could teach us writers quite a bit about letting go of inhibitions and speaking from the heart. After all, isn't that what good writing really is all about?

One year Moore mentioned he was acting in an upcoming movie, "Lucky Numbers." Although he had made several movies and often appeared as the determined interviewer, "Lucky Numbers" marked his first role acting as someone other than himself. The reporter in me knew this was news I couldn't ignore.

That night at dinner, I stopped by his table and asked if I might interview him about his upcoming movie role. I instantly sensed his inhibitions and protective shield coming up. I was no longer just another writer but I was one of "those" writers.

His wife spoke up and smoothed it over. She gave me the name and number of his publicist, and when the movie was released, I made the call and received my phone interview with Moore.

"It was really fun and a lot easier than making a movie," Moore told me. "You just show up, read your lines and leave. I can see why people like this life."

Gillian Anderson, star of television's "X-Files," spent a few of her growing up years in Grand Rapids, graduating from City High School in 1986. During the run of the television show, 1993-2002, Press television reporter Ruth Butler did several interviews with her. But I didn't catch up with Anderson until five years after the show closed. Anderson was a mother of two, living in London and awaiting the final script for the television show's second big-screen version, "The X-Files: I Want to Believe." She had come to Grand Rapids to visit her mother and grandmother, and spoke at a fundraiser for the fight against neurofibromatosis, a genetic disorder that her brother has.

"In England, we raised $150,000 last year for NF, " she said.

Anderson supports many charities, including a variety of causes in Africa.

"It's an unexpected benefit of celebrity," she said. "I discovered the benefits of someone who is in the public eye pointing attention to something that needs attention."

She and fans of "The X-Files" raised the money to build a school in Uganda. She spoke excitedly about developments most of us take for granted, such as getting the school on the electric grid or raising enough money for a borehole so the community could have fresh water.

"It's been an extraordinary experience," she said. "Over the years, 'X-Files' fans have donated money and gotten involved in raising money and started to volunteer because they see me volunteer."

I also tried to keep in touch with Elizabeth Wilson, who grew up in Grand Rapids and started acting at Grand Rapids Civic Theatre. Her name may not ring bells, but you'd recognize her face. She was Dustin Hoffman's mother in "The Graduate" and a school representative in the movie version of "The Addams Family." She also has a long Broadway resume. She debuted in "Picnic" in 1953 with Paul Newman, and was most recently seen in "Waiting in the Wings" in 1999-2000, when she was almost 80 years old.

Wilson, who is close to 90 as I write this, has a wonderfully friendly personality and speaks so casually about the actors she's worked with. She calls Lauren Bacall by her nickname, Betty.

"People think of her as being aloof but she's not," Wilson recalled. "She always gives a lot and makes herself available. She was only 33 when Humphrey Bogart died. Widowed with two sons at 33. She's a tough girl."

Elizabeth Wilson (with scarf) visited Grand Rapids in 2004 during Circle Theatre's production of "Morning's at Seven." She's pictured with cast members Bernice Houseward, Marney MacAdam and Sheri-Beth Dusek.

Wilson also recalled Paul Newman visiting her dressing room when they were in "Picnic."

"I had never seen eyes like that," Wilson said leaning forward like a teenager sharing a secret. "I remember having to look away, his eyes were so gorgeous."

In 2007 she was inducted into the Theatre Hall of Fame, which she said was more exciting than winning the Tony Award in 1972 for "Sticks and Bones."

"I guess it's the name, 'Hall of Fame,' and that it honors all of your work."

Broadway choreographer Jerry Mitchell grew up in the southwestern Michigan town of PawPaw, and chatted with me often about his Tony Award nominations. In 2005, when he was nominated for the choreography of "Dirty Rotten Scoundrels" and "La Cage Aux Folles," he came back to Michigan the day before the Tony Awards broadcast to attend his nephew's high school graduation. Then he rushed back to the Big Apple to accept the award for "La Cage."

"I come from this little town where everybody knows everybody," he told me. "Now 25 years later, I live in one of the biggest cities in the world. But I go to these award shows, and I look out and see all these people I've worked with in other shows, and it doesn't seem much different from PawPaw. Theater is a tiny town."

All That Nunsense

Nuns have brought a lot of nonsense to the stage. Michigan native Dan Goggin is responsible for most of it—a series of six "Nunsense" plays featuring the same five silly sisters in one fund-raising fiasco after another. More recently, Chicago's Maripat Donavan has added to the habit parade with the "Late Nite Catechism" series. Both revive the Catholic experiences of an earlier time, when nuns wore black-and-white habits and demanded the kind of "Yes, Sister" respect that is almost laughable today.

Attending a Catholic School in Alma, Michigan., Dan Goggin noticed everything was funnier when the nuns did it. Shapeless black-and-white habits made nuns look like penguins bobbing around on the playground, he told me. That memory inspired Goggin's enormously popular 1984 musical, "Nunsense," which multiplied into a series of six plays from the Christmas version, "Nuncrackers" to the latest, "Nunsensations," a Vegas revue with hot-pink feathered fans complementing the habits. With only five cast members and simple black-and-white costumes, the plays were easy for community theaters to put on, and pretty soon every community theater was doing one of the "Nunsense" shows. I remember David Nicolette, my predecessor, complaining that he didn't want to review yet another production of "Nunsense."

But when the 20th anniversary tour came to Grand Rapids in 2004, I was tickled to cover it because the cast was packed with stars: Kaye Ballard, Georgia Engel, Lee Meriwether, Mimi Hines and Darlene Love.

Ballard, who's probably best remembered for the 1967 television show "The Mothers-in-Law," will go down in my memory book as the funniest phone interview I ever did. Every response to every question was a punchline. I caught up with her when "Nunsense" was performing in her hometown, Cleveland.

"I've got like 100,000 relatives here," she said, before modifying the tally to two sisters, a brother and their offspring.

One problem of performing in her hometown was they knew the truth. Ballard, 78 at the time, was one year older than her bio.

"I lied for years," she said. "What good is a year? I should have taken off five."

She even joked about being born the same day as Robert Kennedy.

"I guess I'm lucky to be here and still working."

I remembered her as one of the stepsisters in the television version of "Rodgers and Hammerstein's Cinderella" as well as "The Steve Allen Comedy Hour." But she was a recording artist and stage star as well.

"I should have done more television," she quipped. "When you're on television, you're everybody's friend. When you're not on television, people think you're dead."

Georgia Engel also was a delight to interview. The ditzy blonde from "The Mary Tyler Moore Show," and more recently "Everybody Loves Raymond," was every bit the innocent airhead in person that she is on the television shows. That breathy, helium-high voice isn't an act.

"To my ears, my voice doesn't sound any different than other people's," she told me. "I guess we don't hear ourselves the same."

I joined Engel and Lee Meriwether when the cast lunched with the Grand Rapids Dominicans at Marywood, a convent and retirement facility where many of the nuns of Goggin's childhood lived. Engel is just as sweet and friendly as you would expect. She bowed her head in prayer with her tablemates, and when one of the real nuns mentioned she'd forgotten to get a piece of fruit, Engle quickly jumped up and retrieved an orange from the buffet for her.

I dined at a small table with four nuns and Meriwether, a former Miss America who was a regular on the "Barnaby Jones" television series in the 1970s. Meriwether and the nuns chatted like old friends, comparing their stage experience as if a nun's memory of being in an eighth-grade production of "Our Town" had any comparison to Meriwether's appearance in a Broadway tour or television episode. Yet, when a nun's quip broke up the table in laughter, Meriwether was quick to compliment her comic timing.

I got another opportunity to visit with Engle a year later when Goggin debuted "Nunsensations" at Mason Street Warehouse in Saugatuck, a Lake Michigan resort town and art colony. I watched as she rehearsed one of the dance numbers, and although her face seemed as clueless as ever, she flawlessly followed complicated directions and worked together with the other dancers. She may sound silly, but you soon realize she has to be quite smart to pull it off so well.

After the rehearsal, Engle and I sat in the theater seats chatting about the new show. Engle saw the nuns as being naïve, the embodiment of the innocence that's always central to the characters she portrays.

"The nuns are in foreign territory," she said of the Vegas revue."They're in awe of the place. My favorite line is 'From high atop the third floor of the Mystique Motor Lodge.' They think they've hit the big time," she said, bursting with laughter.

Engle's father was born in Grand Rapids, so while she was in Michigan she spent some time visiting the area where her grandparents had lived, which she hadn't seen since childhood. But as you might expect of one of her vacuous characters, Engle couldn't tell me the name of the street or even the neighborhood where they lived. Her sister, who was coming to see the show, was taking care of all those details, she said.

On the opposite end of the spectrum, nuns are infinitely wise in Maripat Donovan's "Late Nite Catechism" series.

"To portray nuns as inept or stupid is very incorrect," Donovan told me when the original "Late Nite" show came to Grand Rapids' Circle Theatre in 2004. "Nuns are able to take care of themselves and us, too. They are nurses, social workers, deans of colleges. They take care of us in the hospital when we are born and in the nursing homes when we are old. They take care of the whole world."

The "Late Nite" series recreates Catholic education as Donovan remembers it. The theater is transformed into a '60s classroom with blackboard and prayer cards. Audience members are students in a crash course under the tutelage of one very determined, habit-clad Sister, who carries a ruler to rap a few knuckles if audience members aren't paying attention. Although she peppers her lessons about the Bible and the saints with lots of witticisms, latecomers take their life in their hands. She publicly embarrasses anyone who dares to chew gum or wear a short skirt.

The original show was so popular that many actresses have been hired to play the part of Sister. Long-running productions were going on in several cities in addition to the professional tour that came to Grand Rapids. Donovan decided to add a Christmas version, which she personally field-tested in the basement fellowship hall of Sacred Heart of Jesus Catholic Church in Grand Rapids.

What a surreal experience! Donovan set up her stage at one end of the hall, which was filled with real nuns, priests and parishioners sitting on folding chairs and munching homemade cookies from paper-covered tables set up at the back of the room. Her stage area was spread across the end of the room that led to the restrooms. In the middle of the show, an audience member headed to the bathroom and she turned him into a laughingstock. Not surprisingly, no one else needed to go until intermission.

"I couldn't have asked for a more perfect place to debut the show," Donovan said.

"We needed a low-pressure first audience."

I can't believe what an opportunity it was to see the show in its developmental stages, presented in the actual setting that would be depicted a month later on the Gem Theater stage in Detroit and in a touring show that came to Grand Rapids a year after that. The series went on to add a third show, about wedding vows, which also played to packed houses in Circle Theatre a few years later.

But the world premiere of "Sister's Christmas Catechism" was pretty much a secret between me and the lucky parishioners of Sacred Heart of Jesus, except for a brief mention in the Stagehands column in The Press. The newspaper wasn't interested in a review or any coverage of the event because it was just something in a church basement, not a "real performance."

I don't know how it could get more real.

You Raise Me Up

When people ask me for my favorite star story, I think of singer Josh Groban and the ultimate fan, Connie McDonald.

A classical crossover star whose hits are likely to be in Italian or Spanish as often as English, Groban sang in the closing ceremonies of the 2002 Winter Olympics, and within a year, his first album had sold four million copies. When I first read about him in People magazine, he was packing arenas, even though no one seemed to know how to classify his repertoire.

One phrase in the magazine's story jumped out at me —"Grand Rapids, Mi., dental office." The local reference stopped me and I reread it. The fan being quoted in this story was from Grand Rapids and worked in a local dental office. I knew this had the potential to be important someday, so I e-mailed my boss, Entertainment Editor John Gonzalez, and gave him the name. If Groban ever came to Grand Rapids, whoever was doing the story would want to talk to this fan. Then I promptly forgot all about it.

Well, Groban's tour came to Grand Rapids a couple of years later, in February 2005, and I don't have to tell you that neither John nor I had kept track of that fan's name. To complicate matters, Groban didn't fit any of the usual "beats." He wasn't rock or classic rock or any kind of pop that you would hear on the radio, so none of our popular music reviewers was interested in covering him. And Jeff Kaczmarczyk, who covered symphony and opera, didn't feel Groban met classical music standards, either.

Groban just packed arenas.

My friend, education reporter Kym Reinstadler, was a fan of Groban, so I volunteered to cover the concert, knowing she would love to see it and I could always educate myself on this singer's music.

I gathered all the CDs and DVDs of his performances and read everything I could find, including interviews and reviews of the current tour. Then I contacted the publicist and arranged a phone interview. I tried to track down the lost People magazine story online but didn't have any luck. Then I got an idea. I called my dentist's office. The receptionist knew me well enough to trust me. Of course, it was too much to expect that she would know the dental office employee mentioned in People magazine, but she put me in touch with the president of the local group of dental office managers. As soon as I mentioned Josh Groban, the group president knew exactly which fan I was talking about. Connie McDonald.

Connie was fanatical. She had flown all over the United States and Canada to see Groban perform. In 2003, when his fame was just beginning, she believed in him so much that she would buy a few extra albums and pass them out to flight attendants, taxi drivers, her doctors...anyone to spread the word.

"I felt like it was my calling," she said when I visited her home. "He has a voice that really grabs you."

But when I met Connie I couldn't believe my eyes. She was in a wheelchair. Cancerous tumors on her spine had left her partially paralyzed. Besides working as an office manager for a local dentist, the 60-year-old divorced mother of three had pretty much stayed home for years, she said. Groban gave her the inspiration she needed to stretch outside her comfort zone. She drove all the way to Cleveland to meet the singer for the first time and get a CD autographed. Then she flew to New York and took a taxi to NBC's "Today" show just because he was going to be on. That kind of traveling would require extraordinary devotion from any of us, but for a woman who had never tried to navigate an airport in a wheelchair, never been to New York, or never tried to flag a taxi, it was courageous.

"It's gotten her back in the flow," one of her daughters told me. "She's back having fun like she did before the wheelchair."

The 2005 concert at Van Andel Arena in Grand Rapids was the 64th time McDonald had seen Groban perform. The artist couldn't help but notice her.

"Thank God for Connie McDonald," Groban told me in a phone interview. "She's been there from day one. She's a diehard fan. You can't take for granted the people who believe in you."

He recalled the times she went to New York just to see him on "Today."

"It would be blistering cold outside and she'd be outside the window in her wheelchair and a blanket," he said. "And I'm thinking to myself, 'I appreciate her support, but she's got to be getting tired of this.'"

When she had surgery and missed a concert or two, Groban and his parents sent her a get-well basket, "From your fan club."

I have to admit, Groban is easy to fall in love with, though my friend Kym is still laughing that I described him as a "bottomless baritone" in my review of his 2005 concert. Let's just say he has a rich voice with a broad range and an effervescent personality. Perhaps I feel drawn to his music because he's really a musical theater performer. He emotes a song so you understand it even when you can't tell for sure whether he's singing in Italian or Spanish. A song is so much more than the words.

"I want to widen what pop is rather than change what classical is," he said. "I absolutely want to sing songs that I can sing with all of my heart. A song I sing has to be something I can connect with. No matter how many times I hear it, it gets me every time."

Nobody had to ask me twice to review his 2007 concert, and I often play his CDs just for fun now, even when I'm not preparing for an interview. In some ways, I prefer the music on CD. The concerts often are overdone with special effects. The 2007 concert featured one of his original works, "February Song," which was quite lovely when he did it on "Today" with no special effects. At the concert, a video seascape of waves rippling to shore provided an appropriate backdrop, but as the music built, the video changed into a view of outer space, then a meteor shower and a climactic, overwhelming white light reminiscent of a scene from "Close Encounters of the Third Kind." Way too much.

As I pointed out in my review, sincerity works better for Groban than spectacle: *"Groban had the crowd eating out of his hand when he sat on the edge of the stage, signed a few autographs and then sang a very intimate number, 'Not While I'm Around,' from the Stephen Sondheim musical, 'Sweeney Todd.'"*

But beyond his extraordinary performances and chatty interviews, I appreciate Groban because he appreciates his fans.

Connie, who called herself his roadmom, died about seven months after the 2005 concert. Grobanites, the friends she had made among his fans, came from all over the country for her funeral.

"She's every artist's dream as a fan, and she's every person's dream as a friend," Groban said when contacted by phone. "She inspired not only me but everyone she came in contact with. The hardest news for me was finding out the cancer had returned…and she was in pain. But she greeted death the way she greeted life, with dignity and strength."

Now when I hear Josh Groban singing his 2003 hit, "You Raise Me Up," I think of Connie McDonald and wonder who inspired whom.

Pretty in Pink

Of all the stars I've interviewed, only one made my daughter-in-law's eyes light up: Molly Ringwald.

Molly was the darling of the generation that came of age with her movies:"The Breakfast Club," "Sixteen Candles" and "Pretty in Pink." With her faintly freckled face and auburn hair, she reminds me enough of my daughter-in-law, Angela, that I can't help but call her by her first name.

Molly's star was twinkling everywhere in the 1980s but had faded quite a bit by the time she came to Michigan with the Broadway tour of "Sweet Charity" in 2007. I met her in a stark, concrete-walled meeting room in East Lansing's Wharton Center, where she was appearing in "Sweet Charity" before bringing the tour to Grand Rapids.

As Tony Curtis had done, she dressed to be photographed only from the waist up. The deep folds of a black, Issey Miyake jacket framed her familiar face, auburn curls and big brown eyes. But the fancy jacket was worn over a loose, black knit dress that hung as limply as an oversized T-shirt. Below, her legs were bare, her feet in gold sandals, and a large bandage on one toe.

"I fractured it," she said as we waited for the photographer to set up her camera. "I'm not sure exactly when it happened. It wasn't on stage. I just bumped into something and vaguely remember going, 'Ow, that hurt.'"

Surprisingly, the attractive actress was camera shy and didn't want our photographer to take photos while she was talking to me, so I tried to make small talk during the first five minutes of our 15-minute interview time, while the photographer set up camera angles and tested the lighting.

The daughter of blind jazz pianist Robert Scott Ringwald, Molly told me she wanted to grow up to be a black jazz singer.

"That's the people I admired. I grew up listening to Bessie Smith and Ella Fitzgerald. I thought eventually my skin would get darker. I didn't know how I was going to get there, I just thought it would happen."

Molly was traveling with her fiancé, Panio Gianopoulos, and their 3-year-old daughter, Mathilda, who Molly said was as big a ham as she was as a child. But she said she plans to keep her daughter away from performing until she's an adult.

"I want her to have a normal childhood; just have fun," Molly said. "I feel bad for child actors. It really is a big business. My parents didn't know that side of it. But knowing what I know, I don't want her to be a child actress. It's my story. It doesn't have to be her story."

Tucked into that colorless interview room, Molly was gracious and enthusiastic discussing the show. She also was eager to turn the interview into a more casual conversation, asking me about my job and inquiring about entertainment options in Grand Rapids.

When the publicist came in at the end of our 15-minute interview slot, I'd probably had less than 10 minutes of actual interview time. Since the photographer and I had each driven for more than an hour to East Lansing, we wanted more than a combined 15 minutes, so I asked the publicist if I might observe another interview from the background. I received permission from the next appointment, a television station, to sit in. I wasn't going to ask any questions, but it would give me another chance to observe Molly's mannerisms and hear her answers to another reporter's questions. I always wanted to give my readers the best possible story, and you never knew what might happen in the next 10 minutes that may be so much better than what happened during the past 10 minutes.

Molly agreed at first, but then changed her mind without warning and asked to have me escorted out of the room before the television cameraman was finished setting up. I was disappointed. She was almost 40, but in some ways still behaved like a petulant teen.

"Sweet Charity" was somewhat disappointing, as well, but I'm not sure it was Molly's fault. I mean she wore one red dress through the entire show. Hey, big spender! You think you could spend a little cash to add some flash to your star?

And though she did an adequate job of singing and dancing, she's not a snappy dancer like Gwen Verdon, for whom the role was written. So, duh, don't stick her out on the stage for a prolonged solo dance routine.

Molly did, however, prove to be outstanding at physical comedy. In one scene, in which Charity is locked in a closet, her comic faces reminded me of another redhead, Lucille Ball. A better director would have found ways to play up the star's assets instead of expecting her to play the role as originally written.

Country Fan

I didn't start out being a country music fan, but somehow after I went through my divorce in 1982, the sad stories and plucky attitude of "today's country" hit a chord with me. That was about the time the band Alabama rocketed to No. 1 with a drum-driven sound that was more rock than country music had ever been. The rock stations were playing heavy metal, and I discovered rock as I knew it had moved to the country stations.

I became a big Alabama fan. I had every album, several T-shirts and went to concerts whenever the band came within 100 miles. They were The Beatles of my 30s and 40s, my midlife mania. But I never thought about interviewing a member of the band or reviewing a show. Somehow it seemed too close, too personal. What journalists call a conflict of interest.

I remember when I was entertainment editor for The Grand Rapids Press and John Gonzalez was our rock music reviewer (yes, the same John Gonzalez who later became entertainment editor and my boss when the tables were turned.) John was reviewing Alabama at the Ionia Free Fair and I was just a screaming, black-T-shirt-wearing fan in the crowd, taking the day off from being his boss. I thought it was a great concert, although I was disappointed in the encore, which was a Motown medley, sort of a tribute to the Michigan audience instead of the usual Alabama fare. I had never been a Motown fan—or a Michigander—so I would have preferred more of my Alabama favorites.

In the review, John raved about the encore as the best part of the show, probably the only songs he liked or felt really familiar with. And that's the problem of reviews. It always depends on your perspective.

When Alabama came to the Allegan County Fair in 1996, I volunteered to do the advance interview even though I still was an editor at that point and writing wasn't my job. But I enjoyed talking with Teddy Gentry about the band's history, which I knew very well, and laughing about things that happened at concerts I had attended. It's no wonder Alabama's music appeals to the common man.

"That's because we've been there, done that," Gentry told me. "Hard work, that's how we were raised. I'll never forget what it is like to get up at 4 or 5 in the morning and work all day and come home dog-tired and then get up and do it again. You don't forget what it was like. That's the reality of living."

For me, interviewing a musician is entirely different from talking to an actor, because I relate to the work on a different level. But after I switched hats in 2000 and became a full-time entertainment writer instead of an entertainment editor, my interest in country music as well as Irish music and dance broadened my coverage area beyond theater.

I reviewed packed arena concerts for such country stars as Alan Jackson and Kenny Chesney, sometimes on deadlines so tight that I would sit in The Press box high above the stage, typing during the show and hitting the send button just before the encore. There was no time to check a song title or look up who recorded that song originally in what year. You have to rely simply on what you know in your gut.

Three times I headed up the team that covered the B-93 Birthday Bash, a free, two-day country music festival sponsored by Grand Rapids country radio WBCT-FM. I had attended the show several times as a fan, squeezing up to the front row the year Alabama played the final set at the Allegan County Fairgrounds.

But covering the show is a whole different animal, and frankly, no fun. You've got to deal with computer connections that are iffy at best and deadlines that seem impossible to meet. And worst of all, you have hours and hours of performances to summarize in a few inches of copy. In 2000, when I covered the Bash in Allegan, my connection to the Internet was a wire dangling from a pole in the middle of a field and I just had to pray that the technology gods somehow would allow the story to make it through on time. Technology improved by the time I covered the Bash in Ionia in 2007 and 2008. With AT&T as one of the sponsors, we supposedly had WiFi, but that, too, was iffy. I kept carrying my computer around, trying to find the spot where it would work. Finally, right on deadline, the signal went away and I went rapping on the door of the trailer where the radio station was hooked up and demanded help, which I'm grateful to say they supplied.

B-93 was a great host to The Press, even though the sheer size of the project often led to problems. One year, the station gave us a trailer in which to set up our computers. It was supposed to be air conditioned, but the air conditioning couldn't keep up with the heat wave, and it was an oven instead. Actually a smelly oven, because there was a toilet in the trailer that backed up.

We spent much of the day trying to figure out who that year's surprise guest would be. Surprises are a problem for a reporter on deadline because it takes a lot of research to do a good interview and ask pertinent questions. I was delighted when word leaked out that the guest would be Clint Black, an artist I had been following for years. A meet-and-greet had been set up with fans who had won an on-air contest, so I chatted with them as they lined up to meet Black and hoped he would spare me a few words at the end of the line. As it turned out, he welcomed me into his trailer, and we were able to chat for quite a while. The highlight of Black's set was his newest song, "The Strong One," about single mothers. Having lived that life myself, the song really rang true to me.

"Women who are doing it alone, know how it is," Black told me. "But I think guys will like (the song) too."

Jessica Simpson was the surprise guest the following year. The sexy Daisy Duke from "The Dukes of Hazzard" movie was at Bash to promote her first country single, "Come On Over." The surprise was she didn't even try to sing it; she just stood around while a recorded version played over the loudspeakers.

Simpson was so shy of reporters that our team was no longer allowed backstage on the day she was to appear. The radio station moved us to a nearby motel room, which turned out to be the best camp yet for covering Bash—reliable Internet, air conditioning, and toilets that worked. There was a little time lost walking back and forth between the motel and the show, so we had to choose what to cover and what to miss while we were writing and sending stories, but overall a great solution.

Still, it didn't make Jessica Simpson's no-performance appearance worthwhile.

I was about to retire when Bash came around in 2009, so I was relieved that John Gonzalez didn't ask me to cover it. That is, until I heard the news. The Grand River, which flows past the Ionia Fairgrounds, flooded and trapped more than 1,400 parked cars while people were attending Birthday Bash. The show closed early and some people were lucky to be able to wade out of the mess at all. It was such a big story that many of us in the department—including me—were needed to cover the developments throughout the next week until the cars could be removed. I can't imagine a bigger splash for my last Bash.

My love of all things Irish also opened the door to covering the numerous step-dancing shows such as "Riverdance," "Lord of the Dance" and "Celtic Tiger," as well as Irish music including High Kings, Celtic Thunder, Celtic Woman and, of course, The Chieftains. The latter is my unabashed favorite because the group is so traditional. A Chieftains concert is not lost in smoke and lights as many modern concerts are.

"The music we play is a living thing going back centuries," Paddy Maloney, spokesman for the Chieftains, told me in a phone interview. "It's a part of who we are. God gave us a gift, the members of the group, and we must play for people."

Talking to Maloney was one of the greatest opportunities of my life, though it was a challenge to keep up with the brogue dancing off his tongue faster than an Irish jig. At times like this, when I'm talking to someone I admire like Paddy Maloney or Clint Black, I feel the huge obligation I have as a writer to capture that moment in a few words and share it with my readers.

One Brief Shining Moment

"Camelot" has come to symbolize those ideal moments that fade away too quickly but are never forgotten. The musical has been touring for almost 50 years, shining with varying degrees of success on many careers.

I was entertainment editor in 1994 when Broadway Theatre Guild brought "Camelot" to Grand Rapids with debonair crooner Robert Goulet as King Arthur. Goulet had launched his Broadway career as Sir Lancelot when Lerner and Loewe's "Camelot" debuted in 1960, so it was a little ironic that the impetuous youth who stole Guenevere's love should become the wronged king 34 years later.

Goulet was 60 when he visited Grand Rapids in 1994 and had recently undergone surgery for prostate cancer. I overheard David Nicolette's phone interview with Goulet as they discussed the operation's effect on actor's sexual prowess. I'm not sure that's a line of questioning I would have been willing to pursue.

But I did get my chance to interview Goulet eight years later, when he was touring with "South Pacific." In the wake of the terrorist attacks of 2001, the country was riding a wave of patriotism, and Goulet's website featured a flag-waving patriotic salute. I thought it was sort of funny, considering Goulet received some flak early in his career for messing up the words when he sang the national anthem. The excuse at the time was that Goulet had grown up in Canada, so I thought he was Canadian, but he corrected me. Although his parents were French Canadian, and he lived there from age 13 to 26, he was born in Massachusetts, technically an American.

"I would like to have dual citizenship with Canada," he said.

A few months after that interview, I received a photo Christmas card from Goulet and his wife Vera. But getting on the Goulet Christmas card list hardly is a sign of intimate affection. Goulet's business manager wife sent out 200,000 cards a year to media and other contacts. I continued to receive the annual missive until Goulet's death in 2007.

"Camelot" returned to Grand Rapids in 2008 with Lou Diamond Phillips wearing the crown. Better known for the movies of his early career—"La Bamba" and "Young Guns"—Phillips earned a 1996 Tony Award nomination for "The King and I." The dark good looks of his Filipino/Cherokee heritage won him many ethnic roles, but he told me his heritage shouldn't prevent him from portraying a British king.

"If I were limited by DNA, I'd be out of work," he said. "Many people who aren't Asians have portrayed Asians—Mickey Rooney, Jonathan Pryce, Yul Brenner. When I teach young actors, I tell them not to try to be the best Latin actor or the best African American actor or the best Asian actor. Let your talent dictate the roles you play."

Phillips was touring with his make-up artist wife, Yvonne Marie, and their baby daughter, Indigo. Grand Rapids costumer Marcia Van Kuiken happened to be touring with "Camelot" as wardrobe supervisor and enjoyed playing with the baby.

"We get baby hugs all the time," she told me. "I love to play tour grandma."

Like Phillips, many of the stars who came to West Michigan have known a previous shining moment of fame for some other role.

Richard Thomas became famous saying "Goodnight" over and over on the television family drama, "The Waltons." After that Depression-era family said its final "goodnight" in 1978, Thomas went on to various television and stage roles. He came to Grand

Rapids in 2008 with a revival of Reginald Rose's famous 1954 play, "Twelve Angry Men."

"Because I've been on television, a lot of people are familiar with me, but I've never had the chance to perform for them in live theater," he told me. "I love touring. It's a traditional part of the acting life that I've never experienced before. You have an opening night every week. It keeps the show fresh."

A nerve disorder caused Thomas to lose about 50 percent of his hearing when he was 30, but he told me the disability never slowed him down. He performed with tiny hearing aids, and at night, when he took them out, he could sleep without interruption.

"It's heavy snowfall every night," he said. "You don't hear the phone or anything."

Bea Arthur was known as the outspoken feminist in television's "Maude" and the sharp-tongued, domineering one on "The Golden Girls." But when she visited West Michigan in 2004, Arthur told me it's just an act.

"I'm five-foot-nine-and-a-half in my stocking feet and I have this deep voice, so those are the roles I get," she said. "Inside, I'm five-foot with a high voice. I'm really very laid-back."

I interviewed Arthur when she was about to visit Saugatuck's Mason Street Theatre for a fundraiser.

"We all started out in little theaters, regional theaters, summer theater," she said in her trademark husky voice.

It had been more than half a century since her Broadway debut, but at age 81, Arthur was still knocking them dead. Her 90-minute, one-woman show, "Just Between Friends," was sold out and inspired three standing ovations. She was so comfortable and laidback that she did the entire show barefoot.

Five years later, a few months before I retired, Bea Arthur died of cancer. I called Mason Street Artistic Director Kurt Stamm and we talked about her visit.

"She wasn't here that long," he told me, "but it feels like I've lost a friend."

I understand. The connection we feel to some performers isn't always logical. For instance, I've always felt some sort of kinship to John Astin, the bright-eyed comedian who portrayed Gomez in television's "The Addams Family." But I connected to him because for a few years he was married to Patty Duke, my alter ego.

Duke is a couple of years older than me, but I feel like we grew up together. I've been following her career since she was a marvelous Helen Keller in "The Miracle Worker," first on Broadway and then in the 1962 movie. I used to grope around the house with my eyes closed, pretending to be Patty Duke playing Helen Keller. Later, she had a television sitcom in which she played look-alike cousins. It was my favorite show during my high school years. Her character called her father Pop-O, a nickname I adopted for my father and continued calling him by until his death more than 35 years later.

About a month before I retired, I got the chance to interview John Astin, who was appearing in a play in Lansing. It turned out to be a hectic day at The Press. Departments were being rearranged and I was placed temporarily at a phone in the middle of the copy desk, next to copy editor Todd Fettig. The copy desk is a little quieter than the entertainment department, and I was concerned my lengthy interview would disturb him.

Astin and I had a great conversation about his career and his sons with Patty Duke, actors Sean and Mackenzie Astin. I was surprised to see photos of him without the dark hair and bushy mustache he wore in "The Addams Family." He had been bald for many years, he told me, but the mustache, which was gone for a while, had returned. He shaved it when his sons were small, he said, and it frightened them so he's kept it ever since. He even shared a hint for living with a hairy upper lip:

"I learned to sneeze through my mouth so I don't mess up the mustache," he said.

When I hung up, Todd Fettig was staring at me, and I figured I'd been enjoying my visit a little too loudly. Fettig assured me it was okay, and that he'd actually been listening in.

"It's not every day you get to sit next to someone who's talking to Gomez," he quipped.

But for me, interviewing stars has become an everyday occurrence. In addition to performers, I've interviewed best-selling authors such as Sue Grafton, Anna Quindlen and David Baldacci. I've also talked to world-renowned artists, such as Dale Chihuly, whose wild curly locks seem to mirror his whimsical glass creations.

This memoir is not intended to be a compendium of all the famous folks I talked with in a 39-year career. Nor do I intend to diminish the fame of those I have omitted. I'm simply sharing a few of my favorite moments.

But I was shocked, and a little embarrassed, to realize recently that I couldn't remember if I had ever interviewed Christopher Plummer. Can you imagine talking to such a remarkable actor and not remembering it?

The thought hit me on a visit to the Stratford Festival in Canada. Plummer was appearing in "The Tempest," and we heard wonderful things about the production. It was sold out and we weren't able to get tickets, but it reminded me that we had seen him portray King Lear at Stratford several years before. Then, suddenly I wondered if I had ever interviewed him. I remembered he came to Grand Rapids to host a Christmas show with Julie Andrews in Van Andel Arena. I remembered seeing the show and vaguely thought I had written about it, but I didn't remember who I had interviewed. Thank goodness for computer searches. I did interview Plummer in 2002, and judging by the story, he was in a lighthearted mood as he prepared to tour 15 cities with "A Royal Christmas."

"It gets me out of extra responsibilities at home," he told me. "While my dear wife is slaving away in Connecticut, I'll be gadding about on the road in rock-star buses. I've never done that. I'm going to have fun."

Memory is as fleeting as fame.

This is Work?

Imagine, if you will, all the male characters in a play are wearing stereotypical symbols of male potency—a giant cigar, a flagpole, a mini-missile—strapped on like erect codpieces to express their sexual hunger. Then imagine these men doing a country line dance while so adorned.

Is it any wonder I can laugh myself hoarse just doing my job?

This scene from Heritage Theatre Group's 2003 production of the Greek play "Lysistrata" stands out (pun intended) as one of the funniest shows I've ever reviewed. Directed by Angela Peterson, this 2,500-year-old antiwar classic could have been a snooze. It's about a group of women from Athens and Sparta who refuse to have sex with their husbands until the men stop making war. It's a fantastic premise—one that always seems applicable to whichever war is current. But Heritage Theatre specializes in making the classics extra-entertaining by getting to the humorous heart of the matter. Its directors have done this over and over, such as setting "As You Like It" in a timeless rural South somewhere between Colonel Sanders and "Dukes of Hazzard." Or staging a "Taming of the Shrew" that tumbles down the aisles with such energy you fear for your life.

"Lysistrata" included a female character who obviously was played by a man in an extravagant wig, a reliably funny gambit in many plays. Another actor impersonated then president George W. Bush, throwing in some of the famous flubs from his speeches. The show included original music, ranging from sweet ballads to raunchy rap, and outrageous choreography the Greeks never could have imagined.

But even though "Lysistrata" tops my memory list for humor, my review did not approve of all of the additions. I criticized the use of a standup microphone in one song because it didn't work well with a large group of singers. I also found some of the nudity unnecessary and some of the supposedly humorous banter unfunny.

And that's where the job comes in, sorting out what works and what doesn't and explaining why.

My list of favorite shows—"Wicked," "The Full Monty," "Urinetown," "Spamalot,"—pretty much matches up with popular opinion. But some of my personal favorites never made it to mass popularity. One of the funniest shows I ever saw was "The Scarlet Pimpernel" in Grand Rapids' DeVos Performance Hall in 2001.

"This tongue-in-cheek tale takes France's frightening Reign of Terror and turns it into a train of terrible puns, outrageous acting and kitchy costumes," I explained in my review.

"I knew I was in trouble when I started laughing at the first guillotine scene. I don't think it was meant to be funny. Villain William Michaels was singing a semi-serious song about the charms of "Madame Guillotine," but his eyes were so shifty, his villainy so animated and exaggerated that I couldn't help myself.

"The real scene stealers in this show are the fops—Percy and his band of adventurers who pretend to be flamingly effeminate and obsessed with fashion so no one will suspect that they are involved in undercover plots to rescue Frenchmen from the guillotine.

"Their rescues are like scenes from the Keystone Cops, made all the more ridiculous since a couple of the band are disguised as buxom wenches.

"One number, "The Creation of Man," was so funny that the applause literally stopped the show and I thought the audience would demand an encore on the spot. Just try to imagine eight men in pastel animal-print suits doing a minuet sort of dance with scarves and then topping it off with flamboyant hats and a chorus line."

Of course, it's more than outrageous acting and physical humor that makes this show shine in my memory. I love Frank

Wildhorn's soaring, haunting score with Nan Knighton's catchy lyrics. I still play the cast recording from this show more than any other.

The believable love triangle has ensnared me. With all its silliness, the show never makes fun of the pain these three people share. Percy is afraid his new bride Marguerite is a spy for the French. Marguerite is puzzled by Percy's sudden coldness. And Chauvelin, Marguerite's former French lover, wants her back. Granted, it is as sappy as a bodice-ripper romance, but it really pulls you in. The songs are full of passion such as Chauvelin's, "Where's the Girl?"

"In the dark of the morning, I'll warm you, arouse you," he sings in a sensuous purr. OMG, irresistible.

And because the love triangle is believable, the show has suspense. Will Marguerite leave her effeminate husband for virile Chauvelin? Will she discover Percy is the Scarlet Pimpernel and betray him to Chauvelin? Will Chauvelin catch the Pimpernel? The first act ends with a playful riddle song about who can be trusted, and at that point it's really up in the air.

The Grand Rapids show was the final performance of the Broadway tour, so it attracted about 300 groupies from around the country who had been following the show for a year or more. They wore Pimpernel T-shirts, waved red glow-sticks and sang along on the final reprise of "Into the Fire." I usually have a hard time understanding the devotion of fanatical fans who end up seeing the same show dozens of times, but I could watch this one over and over.

I did get to see many shows repeatedly. Good shows, such as "The Full Monty," came to West Michigan first in the Broadway tour and then were picked up by area theaters as the rights became available. "The Full Monty" meets my definition of great theater because it's not only funny, with catchy, hummable music, but it has realistic characters and an uplifting message. It's the story of some out-of-work steelworkers who try to make money with a striptease act.

The finale, when they really do take it all off, is an amazing feat of theatrics and timing. They get down to only their hats covering their privates and in the final instant, as the hats go flying in the air, bright lights are turned on behind them, blinding the audience. This all happened smoothly in the professional touring production I saw at DeVos Performance Hall and at Mason Street Warehouse, a small professional theater in Saugatuck.

But when The Barn Theatre in Augusta did the show, the timing was off just enough that we all got an eyeful. Knowing that wasn't how it was supposed to be made the slip even funnier. At Circle Theatre, a Grand Rapids community theater, the slips were not so much because of timing flaws but because the shape of the stage meant people seated on the side were not blinded by the lights. Afterward, everyone was comparing notes on who saw what, and it created a whole different dimension of humor.

I much prefer witty writing to slapstick, as in Larry Shue's "The Foreigner," which I was privileged to see at Augusta's Barn, Hope Summer Repertory, and Grand Rapids Civic Theatre. The situation is a bit contrived: A pair of Brits vacation at a fishing lodge in Georgia. One claims his buddy doesn't speak English so the country folk won't disturb him. Just the opposite happens. They bare all their secrets because they don't think the foreigner can understand them. Shue's wonderful writing takes it far beyond the silly premise, with hilarious insight into our language and people. And a Southern stooge, who can pronounce "Lamp" with two syllables, doesn't hurt either.

"Urinetown" is another hilarious show I was able to see at Mason Street and Grand Rapids' Actors' Theatre. It's an in-your-face ridiculous comedy about a place where people have to pay to pee, and bodily functions are turned into crimes. It skewers our society, big business and government regulations. The songs are catchy and several scenes are send-ups of "Annie," "Les Mis" and other Broadway musicals.

Not everyone agrees about what is funny. I loved the campy musical "Bat Boy," which I saw at Augusta's Barn and Actors' Theatre. A half-boy, half-bat child is adopted by a family that tries to teach him human language and behavior. Some of it is outrageous silliness, but when I said so in a review, The Press received a letter to the editor complaining the play wasn't funny at all.

"I couldn't help but wonder if Ms. Merrill and I saw the same production! There were almost no funny lines. It clearly was a musical and equally clearly, was not a comedy. It had no comedic content whatever, which is rare for a piece based on such a foolish premise," the letter said.

I was thankful that another letter to the editor came to my defense and pointed out that everyone in the audience was laughing.

Personal experience has a strong effect on people's reaction to a play. I loved Grand Rapids Civic Theatre's production of "Arsenic and Old Lace," partly because I did a reading from the show in high school and partly because I grew up watching the black-and-white, 1941 movie starring Cary Grant on the Late, Late Show. When I saw the show at Civic, I was tickled because it was obvious so many people in the audience had never seen it and were surprised by some of the twists and turns that I had come to expect.

But I found a little surprise for myself as well. One of the lead characters is a theater critic, and I found myself chuckling in a new way at all the comments about my dubious profession.

Last Laugh

I retired one year to the day after The Press printed my most controversial review in which I dared to give the popular sing-along musical, "Mamma Mia!" a failing grade of one star.

The timing was just a coincidence. Honest.

"Mamma Mia!" is a lightweight, silly story wrapped around the '70s and '80s hits of the Swedish rock group, ABBA. A first-year theater student who had never seen the musical or heard of ABBA could tell you that's a recipe for disaster. A good musical, by definition, weaves story and music together. One grows out of the other. You can't take a bunch of songs that were written 20 or 30 years ago for some completely different purpose, tack on a story and call it a musical.

Of course, "Mamma Mia!" isn't the first show to attempt this feat. There are dozens of "jukebox" musicals based on previously popular songs. "Jersey Boys," is an incredibly successful jukebox musical in which the music of Franki Valli and the Four Seasons is used to punctuate the life story of the band members. Most of the songs are used as performance pieces, rather than as a method of furthering the plot, so it works perfectly.

But in "Mamma Mia!," old pop tunes are wedged into a plot about a girl on a Greek island who invites three possible fathers to her wedding. When my review dared to suggest that some songs don't fit the plot, you would have thought I had slammed Jesus, the pope and motherhood.

I wrote my review in 2008 when the wildly popular musical was returning for its second visit to Grand Rapids, right about the time the film version was released. My negative words set off a firestorm of complaints. This show had played to 30 million fans all over the world; fans who end the show on their feet, clapping and singing along for three songs. How dare I imply that all this adoration was misplaced?

The letters were vicious. I was obviously an ABBA-hating witch. The Press should send someone who liked the stage. I should be fired.

The Press received so many complaints that editor Mike Lloyd did a column on the protest. Some of my friends were afraid I was in trouble, being called on the carpet by the editor. But I knew that although Mike didn't necessarily agree with me, he agreed with my right to express my opinion.

He did, however, help me to understand that I had expressed that opinion in a large venue and now it was my job to stop defending my position and let others have their say. As a result, "Mamma Mia!" got more publicity with a one-star review than if I had awarded it three or four stars. In fact, some people from the local theater community teasingly asked if I would give their play a one-star review and start a controversy about their show.

I'm not sorry I took the stand I did, but I do realize it was silly of me to think I could change the world with a review. The world likes "Mamma Mia!" and I don't. That's no different from the worldwide love of coffee, which makes me gag. It doesn't mean that one side is right and the other is wrong.

It's never easy to go against the flow. There are several popular shows I don't like. "The Producers" was the most popular show on Broadway at one time. Give me a break! I can barely tolerate Mel Brooks' offend-everyone style of humor. Yet, when the Broadway tour came to DeVos Performance Hall in 2004, I gave it my first four-star review. I still didn't appreciate the humor, but I enjoyed the performances and the theatricality, and I had to accept that the bulk of the audience was laughing.

I also got skewered anytime I said anything against composer Stephen Sondheim, who is more sacred than ABBA but to an entirely different set of fans. One friend told me that not liking Sondheim was like not liking Picasso. Huh? She implied all reputable art critics appreciate Picasso, and the only people who don't like the artist are those who are woefully ignorant. Ah-ha, so that's how it is.

Another friend agreed and joked that I once described Sondheim's music as having "too many notes." Actually, that was in my review of "Sweeney Todd," and I said "too many parts" as in 10-part harmony instead of four-part harmony. I was looking for some nice way to describe the cacophony, since fans of the form bristle when I describe it as dissonant or chaotic.

I've actually read several books on Sondheim and his techniques, trying to understand the appeal, but it still tastes like coffee to me. I take solace in the fact that several members of the local theater community have told me they don't like Sondheim either. Guess I'm not the only tea drinker.

Sometimes I stray from the pack by liking something that other critics don't. In 2004, I had the opportunity to review the world premiere of Arthur Miller's final play, "Finishing the Picture," at Chicago's Goodman Theatre. The famous playwright was 89 at the time and died a few months later.

I was familiar with Miller's work, including "Death of a Salesman" and "The Crucible." High school and theatre students probe these works, trying to understand Miller's symbolism. I was surprised that most of the other reviewers didn't discuss the symbolism I saw in "Finishing the Picture."

"On the surface, this is the story of a movie production staff trying to coax a depressed star out of bed so filming can be finished," I wrote in my review. *"Though the characters have fictional names, the story closely parallels the 1961 filming of 'The Misfits,' in which star Marilyn Monroe suffered from exhaustion and substance abuse. Miller wrote the screenplay for 'The Misfits' and he and Monroe were nearing the end of their five-year marriage at the time.*

"The real surprise is the comparison Miller draws between a glorious star paralyzed by insecurity and a glorious country whose people are unhappy. Miller makes the comparison in the script a couple of times, and (director Robert) Falls reinforces the idea with projected mountains that morph into a reclining nude."

As in "Death of a Salesman" and "The Crucible," Miller's final play was about much more than the surface story. To me, it was clearly Miller trying to finish the picture he'd been painting his entire career: His impressions of America. "Death of a Salesman" is about the American Dream and how hollow and meaningless it had become. It's not about Willy Lohman, it's about all of us. "The Crucible" is about our melting-pot nation going through a meltdown, not in the Salem witch trials of colonial times, as the plot implies, but in the hateful threat of the McCarthyism era in which it was written.

"Finishing the Picture" compares America to a beautiful sex goddess, giving so willingly of her bounty but weakened by all the demands placed upon her. By the end of the first act, I was giddy with excitement. I couldn't take notes fast enough. It was a fantastic piece of theater to me. But I was disappointed in the days that followed because   other reviewers saw it only as a thinly veiled story about Marilyn Monroe that really didn't add any insight about the actress. There was no reference anywhere to what I thought was the real subject of the play. After Miller's death, the play faded away, never to be produced again, as far as I know.

As for me, I guess I'm finishing my picture too, taking my time and enjoying myself. Even when I stop reviewing for The Press, I'll still be in the theater. As long as there are plays to see, comedies to enjoy, symbolism to probe, I will be in the audience.

Listen and you'll hear me laugh.

My thanks to all the writers, editors and photographers at The Press, some of whom are pictured above on my last day. I'd also like to thank the journalists I worked with in Del Rio, Texas; Charleston, South Carolina; Joliet and Aurora, Illinois. I'm lucky to still be in touch with many of them. I'd especially like to thank former Press copy editor John Phipps, who put his sharp pencil to work on this project, and my son, Ryan Wallace, who handled cover design. It takes more than actors to put on a play and it takes more than writers to put out a paper or book. Thanks for a lifetime of support, encouragement…and laughs.

CPSIA information can be obtained at www.ICGtesting.com
Printed in the USA
BVOW050735150911

271288BV00002B/35/P